"Missional church requires missional people. Period. As simple as that sounds, however, it poses a real challenge for church leaders. *Missional Discipleship* proves helpful for this task. This book identifies and examines key elements for turning members into missionaries."

Dr. Reggie McNeal
Speaker and Author of *Missional Renaissance* and *Get Off Your Donkey!*

"If you'd like to make a genuine connection with the people Jesus misses most—the people formerly known as lost—follow this fascinating cohort of prophetic missionalists who will motivate and educate you to travel to new places."

Dr. Jim Henderson
Founder of ChurchRater.com
Author of *Jim and Casper Go to Church*

"In a day and age where missional discipleship is an endangered species, it's refreshing to see a tenacious work that jealously guards the redemptive heart of Christ—'to be in the world but not of the world.' Maddix and Akkerman bleed for the kingdom, and this book reflects that passion. It reminds us that the local church needs to be incarnational, intentional, and true to the original mission of Christ Jesus."

Rev. Ruben M. Villarreal
Founding Pastor, ThornCreek Church of the Nazarene
Denver

"Discipleship has been something of a Gordian knot for those grappling over how to attain a deeper and more authentic Christian life amid new social and cultural realities. This much-needed book helps pastors and church leaders untie the concepts, methods, practices, and insights needed to make missional and holistic ministry attainable for God's people in the church and in the world."

Bryon K. McLaughlin
Executive Editor of *Grace and Peace Magazine*

"In *Missional Discipleship*, Maddix and Akkerman inspire the church to join Jesus in seeing God's 'kingdom come' and 'will be done, on earth as it is in heaven.'"

Dr. Alan Robinson
National Director of the Brethren in Christ Church, USA

MISSIONAL DISCIPLESHIP

PARTNERS IN GOD'S REDEMPTIVE MISSION

EDITED BY MARK A. MADDIX AND JAY RICHARD AKKERMAN

BEACON HILL PRESS
OF KANSAS CITY

We dedicate this book to the Reverend Jerry R. Carr,
our friend and mascot.
Easter 2013

ABOUT THE EDITORS

Dr. Mark A. Maddix is professor of practical theology and Christian discipleship and dean of the School of Theology and Christian Ministries at Northwest Nazarene University. Dr. Maddix is the coauthor of *Discovering Discipleship: Dynamics of Christian Education, Spiritual Formation: A Wesleyan Paradigm, Pastoral Practices: A Wesleyan Paradigm,* and *Best Practices for Online Education: A Guide for Christian Higher Education.* He has also published many articles and chapters in the areas of Christian education, spiritual formation, pastoral theology, and online education. He lives in Nampa with his wife, Sherri. They have two grown children, Adrienne Maddix Meier and Nathan Maddix, who are both in graduate school.

Dr. Jay Richard Akkerman is professor of pastoral theology, director of graduate theological online education, and codirector of Wesley Center Conferencing at Northwest Nazarene University. A graduate of Asbury Theological Seminary, Nazarene Theological Seminary, and NNU, Dr. Akkerman coedited *Postmodern and Wesleyan: Exploring the Boundaries and Possibilities* in addition to publishing other book chapters and numerous articles. He lives in Nampa, Idaho, with his wife, Kim, and their three daughters, Lauren, Hailey, and Parker.

CONTENTS

PROLOGUE
WHO HIDES A LOBBY ON THE EIGHTH FLOOR?

Jay Richard Akkerman
Northwest Nazarene University

WHICH FLAGSHIP HOTEL hides its lobby eight stories above one of America's busiest pedestrian zones? The answer: New York City's Marriott Marquis.

Designed by famed architect and real estate developer John Portman, the Marriott Marquis is located centrally in the Bowtie of Times Square. But in one of America's busiest intersections with roughly 370,000 pedestrians passing by each day,[1] why would a leading hotel conglomerate squirrel away its lobby so high above the passing throngs?

Quite literally today, New York's Broadway Theater District pulses with energy just beyond the hotel's front doors. Massive video screens wink day and night onto Times Square's neon enclave. But when this fifty-story construction project was first announced in 1972, Times Square had an unsavory reputation. Charles Bagli notes in a recent *New York Times* article that "by the early 1980s, the city and the state were desperate to redevelop Times Square, then a district of T-shirt and X-rated shops and shuttered theaters that many New Yorkers avoided."[2] Investors considered Times Square a risky location. Many suspected that organized crime leaders prospered from the neighborhood's numerous go-go bars and adult theaters.

Portman's own associates frame the story this way:

This 1,892-room convention hotel played a significant role in the revitalization of the theater district. Encompassing a full city block, it externally reinforces the energy of Times Square, while the interior provides a retreat from the activity with its bold, 37-story, soaring lobby filled with trees, plants, shops, and restaurants.[3]

In his book titled *The Devil's Playground: A Century of Pleasure and Profit in Times Square*, James Traub observes that

the Marriott Marquis rapidly became the most hated building in Times Square, indeed, one of the most hated buildings in New York. When the hotel opened in 1985, Paul Goldberger [who served for many years as the architecture critic for *The New Yorker*] described it as "an up-ended concrete bunker," "a sealed environment," and "a hulking, joyless presence."[4]

By contrast, Portman defends his decision to cut off the design from the property's adjacent streetscape, and even perching the lobby of the Marriott Marquis remotely on the eighth floor. He notes that

the context has a lot to do with it. The whole idea in New York was to create an internal lung. To take people out of that congested street, up to this garden on the eighth floor, with all this daylight coming in from the skylights. It was designed as a transition from all the congestion and anxiety.[5]

While Traub joins other critics in asserting that Portman's hotel "ostentatiously turns its giant concrete back on the street,"[6] still others praise the architect and his associates for their inwardly centered design.

Like Manhattan's Marriott Marquis, many Christians today seem detached from their neighboring streets. Too often, we seek to clear our lungs, free from the world's surrounding concerns. This book challenges the notion of some who hold that our church's primary orientation should be inward, with little intentional engagement with the world immediately outside our doors. John Portman perched the lobby of the Marriott Marquis high above the masses below. Followers of Jesus today must resist the temptation of positioning their churches beyond the reach of their neighbors.

If you're weary of thinking of the church as a concrete bunker, then this book is for you. It's time to relocate our lobbies down a few floors, adjacent to the sidewalk. As we do, we'll learn to count the cost with our colleagues and explore what it means to become missional disciples in our world today.

1
MISSIONAL DISCIPLESHIP

Mark A. Maddix
Northwest Nazarene University

CHRISTIAN COMMUNITIES talk about discipleship in a variety of ways. Some view discipleship primarily as catechesis, or what takes place through a local church's educational ministries like Sunday school and Bible studies. Others see discipleship including aspects of spiritual formation such as prayer, Scripture reading, and fasting. While others believe that discipleship is primarily concerned with mentoring others and investing one's life in another. Discipleship includes all of these aspects: catechesis, spiritual formation, Christian nurturing, and mentoring, but it also includes compassionate service and missional engagement, particularly since many of these acts shape and form people as they grow in grace.[1]

Historically the church has embraced all of these approaches as valid forms of discipleship. But Christians often struggle with how discipleship is related to evangelism. Evangelism is viewed as a process of getting someone converted, and discipleship is the process of educating and equipping new believers into becoming faithful disciples of Jesus Christ. Those who emphasize evangelism are often concerned primarily about a person's decision of faith. The focus is on ensuring that person is saved. What sometimes suffers, however, is the longer-term growth that takes place through the process of discipleship. Likewise, Christian educators often focus on aspects of nurture and education without giving emphasis to mission and service. Both approaches to discipleship are limited and call for a more holistic approach to discipleship.

This book is written to address discipleship more holistically by including aspects of evangelism and God's mission in the world. In this book, we use the term *missional discipleship* to reflect on the role of a disciple as someone who is engaged in God's mission in the world. Missional disciples are on a journey, becoming more like Christ, investing their lives in others, and embodying lives of love for others. This view puts the church in a new light and sparks a movement dedicated to engaging every context, particularly local cultures, with a mission-shaped heart.[2] A missional disciple is a follower of the life and teachings of Jesus and is committed to being a witness. Too often, this missional language has been divorced from the local church because it was seen as something only missionaries did—not what Christian disciples do.[3] The focus of this chapter, and this book, is to reconnect the relationship of the church to mission and to provide a theological and practical approach to missional discipleship.

MISSIONAL DISCIPLESHIP

Followers of Jesus Christ are called to be disciples. If we take seriously the missional agenda of the church, we simply cannot be disciples without being missionaries, or *sent ones*. As Alan Hurst states, "For way too long discipleship has been limited to issues relating to our own personal morality and worked out in the context of the four walls of the church with its privatized religion. In doing this, we have severely neglected the mandate to go and make disciples."[4] Christians are called to follow Jesus' mandate to "go and make disciples" (Matt. 28:19). Missional discipleship includes both engaging in mission and being intentional about faithful discipleship. Given this reality, many congregations are refocusing to embed the gospel through acts of compassion, justice, and love of both neighbor and community. This missional church movement is deeply connected to a theology of the church that is expressed in the very nature of God as mission. The very heart of the triune God is mission. In fact, *Missio Dei* simply means the mission of God. The missional pattern of the triune God is captured in the words of Jesus who told his disciples: "As the Father has sent me, I am sending you" (John 20:21). God the Father sent Jesus Christ to redeem all of humanity and creation; Jesus sent the Holy Spirit to empower and guide us; and the triune God sent the church into the world to participate in the new creation. God's mission in the world calls, gathers, and sends the church into the world to participate in God's mission. The nature of the church remains to seek and follow wherever God continues to be active in the world.

This missional character of God is expressed in the love that the Father, Son, and Holy Spirit share toward creation, including us. The church is a sent people, responding to the call of Christ and empowered by the Holy Spirit to go into all nations. The church witnesses to the lordship of Christ and participates with God in the building of the kingdom of God (Matt. 28:19-20). The church is an instrument of God's mission for the redemption of all creation. Christians are instruments of God's mission as redemptive agents in the world. Through our participation in God's mission, God is seeking to restore and redeem all of creation.

It is difficult to develop a definition of missional discipleship given the wide range of ways the term is used. However, for the purpose of this chapter and this book, missional discipleship can be defined in this way: *Missional discipleship represents the missionary nature of the triune God with the purpose of forming congregations to embody the gospel and to equip Christians to participate in the restorative and redemptive mission of God in the world.* This definition gives focus to the nature of God as mission, the role of the church as forming disciples, and the focus of engaging in missional practices that usher in the kingdom of God.

MISSIO DEI: A WESLEYAN APPROACH

Wesleyan-Holiness theology roots the *Missio Dei* in an understanding of grace. God's commitment to love creation and God's gracious identification in the incarnation are central to what has been called John Wesley's "optimism of grace." Because grace entails God's loving and noncoercive presence, it cannot be forced upon us: depriving human beings of freedom is not the nature of God's grace. Instead, grace makes possible the human response, as the Spirit works in us both to communicate love and to begin the process of renewal and character formation in the image of God.

The optimism of grace rests on God acting first. The theological term for this is "prevenience." As Wesley put it, "The Holy Spirit is active in our lives even before we are aware of this activity, drawing us to God." Wesley links together divine initiative and human responsibility, which has been called "co-operant grace" or "responsible grace." Divine-human synergism—in which God acts first and human beings freely respond—is central to Wesleyan theology and practice. First, it reminds us that we are called to cooperate with God in the redemption of humanity and all creation. God is already working, seeking to redeem all of creation, including us. Regardless of a person's religious background or heritage, God is at work, drawing and calling each person to truth and goodness.

Second, a Wesleyan view of prevenient grace has implications for missional discipleship. Because God's Spirit is at work everywhere in the world, we can be assured that the Spirit is already present. Moreover, God's presence in every human life gives each person infinite value as the object of God's caring. Prevenient grace initiates the possibility of crossing borders and knowing others on their terms. God's gracious initiatives provoke us into shouldering the responsibility to engage others where they live, to understand their worldview, and to engage others much like the Creator entered creation through the incarnation with all of its inherent risk and expectant hope.

Third, prevenient grace reminds us that those outside the Christian faith may also have the ability to pursue and engage knowledge, truth, beauty, and goodness. Missional discipleship recognizes that the Holy Spirit is operative in the world. It is not limited only to those who are following Jesus. Human existence is not separated between the sacred and the secular. This robust approach reflects a Wesleyan perspective that is Trinitarian rather than exclusively christological. The Spirit is wider-ranging than the human being's explicit knowledge of God through Christ and goes where Christ is yet to be known. But the Spirit is not independent of the Son. The God who acts through the Spirit is the God who Christ reveals as loving and who seeks out human beings wherever they are. This reality poses a responsibility to translate and interpret spiritual truths for those not yet aware of their presence or power.

Many Christians view the church and the world in opposition. Some Christians believe the primary role of discipleship is only to combat societal evils. Others believe God could not be at work outside the Christian community. However, one of the marks of missional disciples is that they recognize the world is good because God made it that way, and that Christians are called to live "in the world but not of the world." Given that there are destructive evils in the world, Christians must recognize their role to be salt and light in the midst of this darkness. But the call to missional discipleship recognizes that God is at work in the world. Because those from other faiths can know what is good, true, and beautiful, we can all see how God is active through all aspects of life, including films, art, music, business, and technology.

God sent the church into the world to continue the ministry Jesus began. Just as Jesus gave his life for the world, so the church, as the body of Christ, is to be broken and spilled out in love before the world. We are sent out into the world as an embodiment of our calling to be the body of Christ. As the church is being sent out into the world, we recognize that this world is sacred, created good by God. The call to missional discipleship requires a rejection of the sacred-secular dualisms that some Christians embrace. God calls the church into the world so that God can restore and redeem the world. This is God's primary mission: the restoration and renewal of all things.

MISSIONAL DISCIPLESHIP PRACTICES

Often, the call to discipleship has been equated with what we believe about the gospel. In this approach, discipleship is more concerned with defending matters of belief or doctrine. This doesn't mean that these things are not important. On the contrary: they are. But missional discipleship hinges on practice more than upholding a particular body of ideas or propositions. People share meals, serve others, discuss issues of culture in relation to their Christian convictions, and pray without beginning with specific invitations to accept the gospel. In practical terms, evangelism in many circles has stressed belief before belonging: one must accept the gospel before becoming assimilated into the church. Missional engagement reverses the trend, stressing belonging first (often tempered by Christian practices), trusting that belief will follow. The life of missional disciples is marked by their engagement in practicing discipleship in their everyday lives. Discipleship is a lifestyle that is deeply embedded in practicing faith. Missional discipleship often begins with simple acts of hospitality, inviting people to gather and engage in service as well as discussing broader social and cultural concerns. In order to be effective in reaching one's neighbors and engaging the culture with the gospel of Jesus Christ, missional Christians understand our essential need to engage in missional practices that are a witness of the good news of the gospel.

Christian practices are a dynamic union with God's mission in the world. They carry an evangelistic weight as a witness to the reality of the reign of God. Missional discipleship is not something that is an add-on or byproduct of the Christian life. Mission is the essence of discipleship. As Kenda Creasy Dean states, "To be little Christs means allowing God to become incarnate in our lives as we smuggle divine grace in the world. Mission simply means translating God's love in human form, putting every cultural tool—stories, symbols, attitudes, language, practices, and patterns of life—at the gospel's disposal."[5] Christian practices are signs of the kingdom of God. They point beyond themselves to the living Jesus, who is the kingdom personified. These practices are a "means of grace" that provide healing and restoration.

A variety of missional practices help bring about a faithful witness to the reign of God. These are more than evangelistic outreach and include acts of compassion, creation care, community development, social justice, and acts of mercy. At times missional disciples challenge larger social concerns, taking on projects that merge both global and local domains. These so-called glocal concerns can include such things as child abuse, modern slavery, ethnic reconciliation, advocacy for the homeless, and creation care. Such activities, often associated with the terms "peace" and "justice," reflect a mind-set that engagement against social ills follows after a God who seeks to redeem all of creation—from the social policies that shape human communities to the very fabric of the environment. Missional discipleship invites different people into these struggles, recognizing that both followers of Jesus and those outside the church can be changed as they see Christlikeness borne out through their efforts.[6]

The chapters that follow will provide examples of pastors and local congregations who are engaged in these kinds of missional practices as a witness to what God is doing in their congregations and their communities.

MISSIONAL DISCIPLESHIP PRINCIPLES

As local congregations repurpose themselves to be more missionally engaged, and as faithful followers of Christ gain knowledge and skills in how to be engaged in missional practices, the following provides some missional discipleship principles that can help guide and inform Christians as they engage in missional practices. This is a representative list of principles that are foundational for missional engagement and discipleship.

Missional Contextualization

As we explore how to implement a variety of missional practices, we must first recognize that every context is different. Missional discipleship is always contextualized in a particular environment. Missional practices that work in one context may not thrive in another. Therefore, it is important to remember that missional engagement is to include local engagement where we live. Jesus' Great Commission to "go and make disciples of all nations" is a command to make disciples *in* all nations, not take them *from* all nations. The Great Commission is not about removing disciples from their contexts but about making disciples *within* their contexts. Missional disciples are missionaries wherever God places them. Our mission fields are located in local communities, workplaces, neighborhoods, and particular church communities. By the Spirit's leading, our task is to discern how to make the gospel of Jesus contextual wherever we are. We need to explore how God is working in our communities, and then invest in a dynamic partnership with God in these places.

All Creation Is Redeemed

One of the central missional discipleship principles is the theological view that Christ came to redeem all of humanity and creation. In Mark 16:15 Jesus states, "Go into all the world and proclaim the gospel to the whole creation" (ESV). Mark's Gospel stresses the importance of redeeming all of creation. Jesus ushered in the kingdom of God and calls on us to participate in the redemption of our world. But we often are so concerned with people getting to heaven that we forget about our responsibility to redeem creation. The kingdom of God is both present and future. The good news of the gospel is that Jesus came to usher in the kingdom of God. When we participate in God's mission in the world, we engage in redeeming all things. Sometimes we are so concerned about making it to heaven that we miss the importance of living out God's mission in the world. Many missional disciples are learning to find ways to restore and renew creation through recycling, renewable energies, community gardens, and land regeneration. If we are going to reach our communities with the gospel of Jesus Christ, we have to show that we care about the world in which all of us live. Through our care for everyone and everything around us, perhaps others will recognize God's love for them. In the end, missional disciples hope they will care more about our faith.

Acts of Compassion, Justice, and Mercy

Another principle of missional discipleship includes being concerned about societal injustices. Many missional disciples today are moved with compassion when others are oppressed or experiencing injustice. They understand the importance of reaching their communities by finding ways to end injustice. They take seriously the call of Micah 6:8, which states we are "to act justly and to love mercy and to walk humbly with [our] God." Many missional disciples are engaged in advocating for the poor, the oppressed, and the widow by responding to these tragedies through acts of compassion and mercy.

Hospitality

Missional discipleship often begins with simple acts of engagement. By inviting others to engage in service, as well as discussing broader social and cultural concerns, many missional disciples are crossing borders with those outside the church. In spite of being placed in uncomfortable situations, their willingness to engage others in conversation and dialogue is bearing fruit. Admittedly, the busyness of life today and our tendencies toward rugged individualism have made hospitality more difficult for some Christians in some contexts. By the same token, the absence of authentic hospitality in so many places today can also underscore its impact. Jesus was known for practicing hospitality. For instance, he invited the chief tax collector, Zacchaeus, to join him for dinner. He engaged in conversation with the Samaritan woman at a well. Jesus crossed social cultural boundaries to engage in conversation with those that others had deemed as outcasts. Missional disciples are hospitable to others because they recognize they are created in the image and likeness of Christ. This includes crossing social and religious boundaries to engage in dialogue and discussion with the marginalized of society. If we are going to reach our communities with the gospel of Jesus Christ, it will require us to open up our lives and engage with others.

Cross-Perspectival Dialogue

Missional disciples recognize the importance of engaging in conversation with those who hold other perspectives. This includes engaging in conversations with people from other religious traditions, those who hold different political views, and those with whom we disagree. Being able to listen genuinely and respect others with differing views is essential to missional engagement. Often local churches struggle to provide safe places for dialogue and discussion about difficult cultural issues. The Christian community needs to be a safe place where we can engage in these conversations. Often people are turned off by the church because of our perceived dogmatism. David Kinnaman, president of The Barna Group, says one of the reasons many young adults have an unfavorable view of the church is because "Christians have become more famous for what we oppose, rather than what we are for."[7] Missional engagement includes the willingness to enter into cross-perspectival conversations in order to understand those with differing views and perspectives. This is critical in learning from others and seeing what God is doing in the lives of our neighbors.

Freedom from Bondage and Oppression

The mission of Jesus was to preach the good news to the poor, to free the prisoner, to make the blind see, and to release the oppressed. In Luke 4:18-19, we read Jesus quoting Isaiah 61:1-2: "The Spirit of the Lord is on me, because he has anointed me to proclaim good news to the poor. He has sent me to proclaim freedom for the prisoners and recovery of sight for the blind, to set the oppressed free, to proclaim the year of the Lord's favor." The gospel is a gospel of freedom and liberation of sin and bondage. Missional disciples are called to help others experience healing and renewal through a dynamic partnership with God in helping to liberate people from poverty, to liberate those in bondage, and to release the oppressed.

CONCLUSION

As many congregations develop a broader view of discipleship that incorporates aspects of evangelism and witness, our understanding of missional discipleship provides a more holistic approach to discipleship. As Christians gather to worship the triune God, we are equipped and prepared to engage in God's mission in the world. Missional disciples acknowledge there is no separation between the sacred and the secular; the world God created is good. As we enter into partnership with God's mission, we engage in missional practices that restore and redeem all of creation. These missional practices provide avenues of witness to those outside the church and opportunities for cross-perspectival dialogue and conversation. Missional disciples recognize that God is active in the world and welcome opportunities to go and participate in what God is already doing.

Discussion Questions

1. Given this book's definition of missional discipleship, how are you engaged in missional discipleship? What might be some areas that need further development?

2. Who are the marginalized in your community? How can you and your congregation become more hospitable to them?

3. In what ways are you and your local church engaged in missional practices? What might be some additional ways you can engage in mission with others in your community?

4. Based on the list of missional principles, which ones do you find to be the most challenging? Why?

5. In what ways can we participate in the redeeming of God's creation? What are some specific ways in which you and your congregation can care for our world?

Recommended Readings

Connor, Benjamin T. *Practicing Witness: A Missional Vision of Christian Practices*. Grand Rapids: Eerdmans, 2011.

Helland, Roger, and Leonard Hjalmarson. *Missional Spirituality: Embodying God's Love from the Inside Out*. Downers Grove, IL: InterVarsity Press, 2011.

Hirsch, Alan, and Debra Hirsch. *Untamed: Reactivating a Missional Form of Discipleship*. Grand Rapids: Baker Books, 2010.

Minatrea, Milfred. *Shaped by God's Heart: The Passion and Practices of Missional Churches*. San Francisco: Jossey-Bass, 2004.

Schwanz, Keith, and Joseph Coleson, eds. *Missio Dei: A Wesleyan Understanding*. Kansas City: Beacon Hill Press of Kansas City, 2011.

Van Gelder, Craig. *The Ministry of the Missional Church: A Community Led by the Spirit*. Grand Rapids: Baker Books, 2007.

2

MISSIONAL SERVICE AND COMPASSION

Brian Postlewait and Grant Zweigle
Vancouver, British Columbia

VANCOUVER, BRITISH COLUMBIA, shined for the world to see in the winter of 2010. The Twenty-first Winter Olympiad showcased Vancouver as one of the world's most beautiful cities with sleek, sparkling skyscrapers saluting the majestic snowcapped mountains at the foot of our neighboring ocean inlets. Bordered by lush green rainforests, luxurious homes bow in reply to the rising skyline. Cruise ships filled with passengers returning from Alaskan vacations fill the streets and sample our diverse ethnic fare. Film crews block access to brick-lined streets to film next year's action blockbuster. Our city's three million inhabitants reflect the spectral diversity of the world and for those with eyes to see foreshadow the City that is to come.

In a city like this, many wonder why people would need God—and most live as if they don't.

What the tourists don't see and the media fails to report is Vancouver's underbelly. Some of Canada's poorest neighborhoods loom just a few blocks from where tourists land in the city. As North America's closest port to Asia, Vancouver sadly traffics more than consumer goods and natural resources. Illicit drugs and exploited human cargo often slip beneath our sight. Behind a spectacular wealthy veneer are thousands of men, women, and children hovering just above poverty in North America's most expensive real-estate market. Lack of affordable housing and minuscule vacancy rates drive many into homelessness.

Vancouver may well have the dubious honor of being North America's most unchurched city. Only 2 percent have a church they call home. On any given Sunday, many more Vancouverites run marathons, ski our slopes, kayak our waterways, fill our markets, or head to the arena for an NHL hockey game than gather for worship. Over the years, many a "First Church" has abandoned our infertile soil for greener pastures. Vancouver First Church of the Nazarene is one of the exceptions. Our congregation's struggle to discern its mission in the city is not uncommon. But staying in the neighborhood of our birth was an intentional choice, albeit not an easy decision.

Yet our church is finding ways to survive and thrive in our difficult missional context. As our congregation embraces Christian hospitality, we find concrete ways to express acts of service and compassion. This fundamental Christian practice has two movements as outsiders are invited to become insiders, and insiders are commissioned to become outsiders in loving service to the world around them. All are welcomed to the challenge of becoming disciples who are then sent as apostles in a deeper embrace of the city.[1] This reciprocal movement of welcome and embrace is creating space for a new movement of the Spirit.

SUNDAY MORNING

It's Sunday morning. As we gather for worship, one notices two of our greeters who are newcomers to Canada. A Mission Possible[2] board member hands out bulletins. A Kenyan family sits behind a Canadian man who is funding water projects in and around Nairobi in partnership with Nazarene Compassionate Ministries East Africa.[3] A developmentally disabled man bounds down the center aisle in step with the preservice music, while his mother, who founded a parent support group for adults with mental handicaps, looks on.[4]

Nearby, one might notice several university students from around the Pacific Rim who connected with our church through a Wednesday evening English Conversation Club. One of the students first came into contact with the Church of the Nazarene in Singapore. A woman who teaches English as a second language on Tuesday mornings warmly greets a husband and wife from China who joined her class recently. Three African-Canadian children are joyfully embraced by a Canadian senior they call "Grandpa." Several Filipinos greet each other in their first language. A single mother looks for her son who has found a place among a rowdy row of preteen boys.

As others enter the sanctuary, another man looks for a seat. By day, he oversees community development at an agency that assists women leaving the sex trade. Beside him walks a woman who volunteers at the same agency. She's looking after children whose mothers are in the program.[5] The cochair of the local elementary Parent Advisory Council prays with the worship team.

After the preservice announcements, a man living with mental illness quiets himself before the call to worship. Music in the Tigrinya language from an East African congregation floats upstairs. Later a multicultural Spanish-speaking congregation will gather in this same sanctuary.

No single sociological factor holds these congregants together. Young and old, the men and women who gather for worship week after week are not defined by any single demographic indicator. What holds our congregation together is a shared love for God and a united commitment to extend Jesus' hospitality to our neighbors, broader community, and the wider world. Ours is a church that exists for the life of the world.[6] But the service and compassion that is embodied through the hospitality of Vancouver First Church of the Nazarene is not a program of our church. It is our way of being Christians in the city. Our church's embrace of immigrants and refugees, the sexually exploited and the marginalized, the mentally handicapped and mentally ill, hard-to-employ people and children from broken families, all flows from the love of God shed abroad in our hearts, moving us outward toward friends and neighbors. This is a congregation that does not have to look far to find people in need.

Our congregation values hospitality. We find that as we practice hospitality, many creative acts of service and compassion flow from it. Outsiders seamlessly become insiders and insiders become their friends. As a result we cannot help but become concerned about the needs of our brothers and sisters in Christ. One might say this is a part of our Wesleyan DNA.[7] When John Wesley urged his Methodists to care for the poor, he expected them to be in personal relationships with them.[8] Wesley understood that service and compassion could only be sustained if the people being served were friends, not mere objects of compassion. As a result, compassion and service in our congregation is rooted in the love that emerges as outsiders become insiders and insiders open their lives to friendship with others.

Hospitality is also resident in our denominational DNA. Phineas F. Bresee, founder of the Church of the Nazarene, indicated that gone are the days when a mission is good enough for the poor—not a mission, but a church with a mission. Before planting the Church of the Nazarene in Los Angeles, Bresee left his prestigious Methodist pulpit to serve as chaplain of an urban mission. There he dreamed of a worldwide movement of God among the poorest of the poor in that city. Such a vision would not be possible merely through arms-length charity. This movement of service and compassion required holy hearts and dirty hands—and a commitment to walk alongside people in the midst of their pain and suffering.

WELCOME

When Gwen's family first visited our church, a friendly greeter welcomed them. Gwen asked if she could sit in a pew near the back of the sanctuary since her adult son was autistic. Gwen's son loved the music, and much to his mother's dismay, he began keeping time by rocking back and forth in his seat. To her surprise, there were no frowns or glances of fear, only warm smiles from others in the sanctuary. A few days later she received a call from a member of the church who asked if our church could help her family with anything. That's when Gwen knew our church could be her home.

One year later, Gwen's daughter announced she wanted to be baptized. After meeting with our pastor, Gwen remarked at how sad it was that her autistic son could not be baptized because he did not understand what it meant. To her surprise the pastor said he would be delighted to baptize her son, just as Jesus welcomed all children.

When members of the congregation learned about Gwen's work with a grassroots nonprofit organization, the Parent Support Group for Families of Mentally Handicapped Adults Society, they embraced Gwen's vision and worked with her to organize social events and fundraisers for the society.

Members of the church volunteered to serve on Gwen's board and others today are advocating for their cause. Today several families in Gwen's Parent Support Group regularly attend our church. Outsiders have become insiders and insiders are compassionately serving their new friends.

EMBRACE

While we often think of hospitality as welcoming guests into our comfortable spaces, the other half of hospitality is the task and risk of being welcomed by others. Sometimes this leads us to places and spaces that leave us uncomfortable at first, and often disconcerted. This is the forgotten movement in hospitality. Ironically, it is the movement that Jesus first commanded his disciples to engage in. In Luke's Gospel, Jesus gave his twelve disciples power and authority to cure diseases, and he sent them out to proclaim the kingdom of God and to heal. He instructed them to take nothing for their journey: no staff, no bag, bread, or money—not even any extra underwear! When they were welcomed into a house, Jesus told them to stay there. Where they were not welcomed, they were told to shake the dust off their feet and move along to the next. The Gospels tell us they went through the countryside, bringing the good news and curing diseases everywhere.

It is risky to stay in a neighborhood when the community changes around us. But it is also risky to move into a new community. We fear incoming storms, or the unknown. Dark alleyways, a changing community, new people and places take us out of our comfort zones.

MISSION POSSIBLE

In the 1980s Elizabeth, who was a member of our church, began walking the streets with others and praying for Vancouver's Downtown Eastside. We were known notoriously as Canada's most troubled community. Ironically nestled in the middle of beautiful Vancouver, the Downtown Eastside is known for chronic homelessness and its illicit drug culture. The ultimate skid row, it is a neighborhood where those challenged by disability, mental illness, and addiction fight for survival. But for those with ears to hear, the rhythms of God's grace can be heard in this place. Liz and her friends walked alongside people who were hurting. They came to know their pain and struggle. Their prayers moved them to action. A dream for a holistic ministry of compassion emerged out of their newfound love for their new friends. As a result, Mission Possible is an innovative Nazarene Compassionate Ministry Center providing basic street-level care for those challenged by homelessness today. From friendship to community development, Mission Possible extends its work beyond basic care—creating opportunities for people to build a ladder out of poverty. In the middle of skid row, gardens are emerging, social-purpose businesses are growing, and people who were often written off and stereotyped by society at large are finding a renewed sense of dignity and purpose.

HEAL THE KIDS

The horizon of our church's compassion begins locally but extends globally. After the tragic loss of their young child, Dominic and Marie turned their grief into a passion to help children around the world. Encouraged by Bob, a fellow member, they set out to make a tangible difference. They had no resources or experience—just a heart for others. Traveling outside of Canada they met other Nazarenes in Africa and South America who were working alongside children in need. While clearly outside of their comfort zone, Dominic and Marie founded Heal the Kids to help the unforgettable children they met. With ongoing support from our church, Heal the Kids has funded and facilitated projects that improve the lives of children around the world. Dominic and Marie's passion has captivated our congregation. In addition to funding Heal the Kids projects, we are now striving to send a team to Kenya to assist and learn from our brothers and sisters in Africa.

The average Nazarene congregation has roughly a fifty-year lifespan.[9] In 2012, our congregation celebrates seventy-five years of transformational ministry in Vancouver. Over those years, our neighborhood has changed dramatically. Today over two-thirds of the residents around our church speak a first language other than English. More families are enrolled in sports clubs than Sunday school. The average Canadian views evangelical Christians as either irrelevant or dangerous. Ministry in Vancouver is not easy.

But in the midst of the challenges and changes, our congregation has remained a center of Christian hospitality leading to tangible acts of service and compassion. The ability to navigate our changing challenges requires the gracious work of the Spirit and faithful, obedient responses from God's people. Our church's ability to navigate Vancouver's shifting demographic and social trends is tied to the intuitive and intentional embrace of our people with the inward and outward movement of Christian hospitality. This movement has inspired many small and beautiful acts of service and compassion by our members.

Since graduating from seminary a little over a decade ago, both of us started our pastoral ministries in small, multicultural, urban communities. We learned quickly that many popular church renewal strategies did not offer much to our ministry contexts. But our ministries have been not so much about appropriating new strategies and tactics. Instead, we have recognized how the Spirit of God has been at work in our city long before we arrived. Our calling in many ways is simple: to discern the Spirit, name the assets, and draw attention to the gifts of God's people. We've learned the power of Christian hospitality, not through theological acumen or technical skill, but through the welcome gifts that have been offered to us—through our humble congregations, immigrants, and the broken and poor within our cities.

Now both of us serve in Vancouver, British Columbia. Grant serves as pastor of Vancouver First Church of the Nazarene and Brian as executive director of Mission Possible. We continue to witness to the reality that success in our ministry context is not the story of individual superhero Christians or dynamic programs. It begins with simple acts of hospitality, rooted in a theological vision of the God who welcomes us and sends us into our cities for the sake of the world.

Discussion Questions

1. How is your ministry context similar to or different from Vancouver?

2. Learn to appreciate your community by identifying the assets, capacities, gifts, and abilities that exist already in your church and neighborhood. How might these appreciated attributes contribute to a renewed vision of ministry?

3. Spend some time naming existing and potential partners in ministry. How might greater collaboration with these individuals and organizations increase your church's ability to connect with its neighborhood?

Recommended Readings

Heitzenrater, Richard P. *Wesley and the People Called Methodists*. Nashville: Abingdon Press, 1995.

Jennings, Theodore, Jr. *Good News to the Poor: John Wesley's Evangelical Economics*. Nashville: Abingdon Press, 1990.

Robinson, Anthony B. *Called to Be Church: The Book of Acts for a New Day*. Grand Rapids: Eerdmans, 2006.

Roxburgh, Alan, and Fred Romanuk. *The Missional Leader: Equipping Your Church to Reach a Changing World*. San Francisco: Jossey-Bass, 2006.

Schmemann, Alexander. *For the Life of the World: Sacraments and Orthodoxy*. 2nd rev. and expanded ed. Crestwood, NY: St. Vladimir's Seminary Press, 1982.

Stone, Bryan P. *Evangelism After Christendom: The Theology and Practice of Christian Witness*. Grand Rapids: Brazos Press, 2007.

Internet Resources

"Heal the Kids Project." http://healthekidsproject.wordpress.com/.

"Mission Possible." http://www.mission-possible.ca/.

"The Parent Support Group for Families of Mentally Handicapped Adults Society, Vancouver, BC." http://www.members.shaw.ca/parentsupport/.

"SA Foundation | Servants Anonymous | Fighting Human Slavery and Prostitution." https://safoundation.com/sa_foundation.

About the Authors

Brian Postlewait, an ordained elder in the Church of the Nazarene, serves as executive director of Mission Possible in Vancouver, British Columbia. Under Brian's leadership Mission Possible has become one of the most innovative Christian humanitarian agencies in Vancouver's social sector.

Grant Zweigle is pastor of Vancouver First Church of the Nazarene, Vancouver, British Columbia. Before coming to Vancouver he pastored Beacon Hill Church of the Nazarene in Seattle, Washington.

3

OSAMA BIN LADEN'S PORN
A PARABLE OF MISSIONAL EVANGELISM

Dana R. Hicks
Nampa, Idaho

IN THE WAKE of Osama bin Laden's death on May 1, 2011, in Abbottabad, Pakistan, one of the more stunning revelations was that America's most wanted terrorist had pornography stashed on his computer. To most outside observers, bin Laden's pornography issue fell a notch below his other more evil inclinations. But for those of us who wrestle with what missional evangelism should look like, bin Laden's pornography is a living example of the tension between individual transformation and cultural change.

The modern era was the age of individualism. The theological child of the modern era, Evangelicalism has reflected the values of individualism for many years. Evangelicals are concerned with getting individual souls into heaven by focusing on making personal spiritual decisions. So we use phrases such as "Accept Jesus as your personal Savior" to describe our desire to see faith as more than what we adopt from others. Faith for Evangelicals is personal; it changes us from the inside out. Personal piety and dealing with one's own sin and brokenness is highly valued. This focus on personal commitment has made the Evangelical movement a defining force in American culture.

But there is a shadow side to this individualistic focus. If faith is only about the individual, our expressions of faith quickly become consumeristic. My conversations focus around having my needs met, finding a church that fits me best, participating in a music program that fits my tastes, or youth programs that meet my family's needs. In extreme cases, one could call it spiritual narcissism—getting God involved in my life, but I am still the center of my universe.

In another sense, according to Evangelical practice and theology, our place in the broader world is akin to being a passenger on the *Titanic*: we are a lot less worried about saving the "ship" of this world than we are about getting people into heaven's lifeboats. In the church where I grew up, I was reminded that Jesus taught, "The poor you will always have with you" (Matt. 26:11). The lesson was that we should stop worrying about oppressive systems, racism, and the overall health of our planet since these were futile concerns. Instead, we loved to speculate about the rapture and would reflect with a longing affection for the day Jesus would come and beam us up out of this pathetic world so we didn't have to deal with it anymore.

Until about a few hundred years ago in Western culture, this idea of us being autonomous individuals was an alien notion for most. People tended to understand themselves more in relation to their family, clan, or tribe. This view yet remains in numerous world areas as people live their lives in the context of a community that defines their identity and gives them meaning. For a growing number of Christians today, this recognition of the larger community is shaping their faith in increasing measure. Faith still has value to the individual, especially in the ways in which it transforms—and is transformed by—the community.

In twentieth-century America, various theological movements attempted to rediscover faith less in individual terms, but in social ones. What we now call the social gospel came from theologians like Walter Rauschenbusch who were less concerned with individual transformation and focused instead on the transformation of oppressive systems and helping people become fully human.[1] For Rauschenbusch and others with a heart for the social gospel, addressing issues like greed, crime, alcoholism, racism, education, and health became important means of expressing their Christian discipleship.

In recent years, writers like Lesslie Newbigin have challenged Christians to think of faith not in terms of *either* the individual *or* the betterment of society, but as *both/and*.[2] Faith is for both the individual and the broader society. To illustrate, Newbigin cites God's call to Abraham in Genesis 12:1-3:

> GOD told Abraham: "Leave your country, your family, and your father's home for a land that I will show you. I'll make you a great nation and bless you. I'll make you famous; you'll be a blessing. I'll bless those who bless you; those who curse you I'll curse. All the families of the Earth will be blessed through you." (TM)

A great heresy of monotheism, Newbigin says, is hearing only half of the Abrahamic blessing. Yes, God will bless, make us famous, bless those who bless us, and curse those who curse us. This is Evangelical passion: the transformation of individuals so that our individual lives can be blessed, good, rich, full, and meaningful.

But the second half of the Abrahamic blessing is just as important: "All the families of the Earth will be blessed through you." We are blessed in order to be a blessing. God does his transformative work in us as individuals so we can be the kind of people who take God's grace, love, and goodness to others. Brian McLaren likes to say, "We are never end-users of the gospel."[3] God's blessing, grace, and gospel always come to us on its way to someone else. We are not meant simply to be receptacles of God's blessing. Instead, we are called to be conduits of God's love, grace, and mercy to the rest of the world.

Which brings me back to Osama bin Laden's porn stash. Part of bin Laden's delusion was that through suicide bombers and mass murders, he and his terrorist army were in partnership with Allah's global transformation. Many in the Islamic world supported jihad against the Western world for its infringement on their faith and values.

As a result, Osama bin Laden's pornography is more than just a late-night comedian's joke on television. In the Muslim world, bin Laden preached famously against America's evils. Decrying the immodest dress of American women, he rallied the faithful to redouble his demands for personal piety. But underneath it all, bin Laden's personal life was full of hypocrisy. Trying to change the world without authentic inner transformation smells a lot more like a grab for power than the genuine expressions of a heart living in submission to God.

Missional evangelism believes both aspects are essential. Our own personal sin and brokenness can be healed and transformed by Jesus' cross so we can join God's corporate global agenda. God's hope for the world is what Jesus called "the kingdom of God coming to earth."[4] We're reminded of this whenever we pray as Jesus taught us: "Your kingdom come, your will be done, *on earth as it is in heaven*" (Matt. 6:10, emphasis added). But Jesus' kingdom will generally not come through rallies, protest marches, and legislation. The way Jesus focused on changing the world was by investing his life in twelve people, eleven of whom were radically altered by their profound personal encounter with him. In this regard, evangelism—the individual transformation of people into Jesus' likeness—remains one of the most important tasks of the church.

VIEWS OF EVANGELISM

I have three kids, and like every other parent, I quickly recognized that each one is very, very different from the next. Some kids are stubborn and need lots of discipline. Some kids are adult pleasers and need coaching in how to not be codependent. Every child is unique, with his or her own unique life struggles. Simple parenting formulas don't work. Parenting must be tailored to every child.

God's children are also like this. One of the most important realizations of the last decade is that discipleship is not a cookie-cutter approach.[5] Because of the infinitely different ways in which we are wired, we learn to be followers of Jesus in a wide variety of ways. What drives to a personal encounter with Jesus is different for every person. Over many years in pastoral ministry, the people I have observed choosing to follow Jesus tend to fall into at least four categories:

Personal Crisis

Ken was married to a woman who attended my church, but he had very little interest in God or spiritual things. When Ken's cousin was killed by a drunk driver, it shook Ken to the core. After his cousin's funeral, Ken and the rest of his cousins went out drinking to drown their sorrows. After a few too many beers, one of them suggested that they pay a visit to the drunk driver who fractured their family.

Neither Ken nor his cousins had a premeditated plan when they showed up at the man's house. But when the now sober drunk driver saw who was at his door and the inebriated state they were in, he locked the door and called the police. This only infuriated the mob even more, so they began to yell and taunt and demand that he come out and face them. Ken had a concealed weapons permit. He pulled his gun and shot into the air two or three times.

The police arrived and arrested the cousins for disturbing the peace. But since Ken had discharged his gun, state law mandated that he had to serve time. Ken was sentenced to six months in the state prison.

I visited Ken during his first week in prison. I was escorted through a maze of jail doors and long concrete hallways to a drab green room where I could talk with Ken privately. When I arrived, Ken was in his prison-issue orange jumpsuit, seated on a rickety folding chair, and flanked by two prison guards. They uncuffed Ken and locked the steel door behind them.

The moment the door slammed shut, Ken buried his face in his hands and began to sob without saying a word. I have never seen a six-foot-three-inch, fully grown man cry like that. When he finally pulled himself together, the first words he said to me were "I need God in my life."

Ken's story is what we typically think of when we think of evangelism—people hit rock bottom and come to realize they need God. It may be a relational crisis, an addiction of some kind, a financial meltdown, or some other major issue. When we come to the end of our ropes, we cry out instinctively to God. In such moments, we hope to discover for ourselves what Eugene Peterson paraphrases in Jesus' beatitudes: "You're blessed when you're at the end of your rope. With less of you there is more of God and his rule" (Matt. 5:3, TM).

But most people we know who are far from God are not having a major life crisis. In fact, their lives may be going quite well. Evangelism for them might require a lot more patience.

Persistent Love

Steve and I met because our kids attended the same preschool. Our wives became friends because our kids played together. After our three-year-olds had a couple of play dates, our wives conspired to have the four of us hang out together.

Steve owned a successful small business. He was a good husband and father. He voted and gave to the United Way. As a young child, his grandmother often took him to her small Presbyterian church for Sunday school. But once he turned ten, he never went back.

Steve and I shared an interest in Major League Baseball and since the Seattle Mariners were making a playoff run that year, it afforded a lot of conversations. Once baseball season ended, however, I had to think of new reasons for Steve and me to get together. I offered to help him remodel his house. As we made our best attempts at home improvements, Steve and I often talked about life, family, and work.

A couple weeks before Easter I told Steve, "Easter is coming up and it's practically un-American to not go to church on Easter Sunday. You should come to our church." He and his family did come, but they didn't come back to church again right away.

Steve and I kept talking baseball and working on his home improvement projects in the months that followed. Over time, they attended our church more and more. It was starting to become a habit. Steve asked me questions about the Bible and issues in his life where he struggled. One day Steve and I were working on his house and I said, "You have been hearing a lot about Jesus the last few months. Do you consider yourself one of his followers?" Steve let his cordless drill drop down to his side and looked past me. He paused and I could see the wheels turning in his head. Then he looked me in the eye and said, "Yeah, I think I am. I don't know when it happened, but I am."

Sometimes people come to Christ slowly. One thing I have learned from my African pastor friends is that Americans are very impatient. Sometimes it takes years of being a spiritual advocate for someone—loving and caring—before that person understands the beauty and goodness of God. Because of our cultural demand to see results quickly, we sometimes give up on what God is doing in another person's life. In Africa, many of the strategies to break into "closed" countries involve fifteen- to twenty-year plans. Sometimes our role in the lives of others is to be a patient and faithful friend.

But some people are not at all passive in their spiritual quest. For some reason they are in full pursuit mode of meaning, purpose, and truth. This was the case with my friend Danya.

The Spiritual Quest

Danya started attending our church because she was dating someone who attended occasionally. Danya grew up in a very conservative Jewish home. Her father lived most of his life in Israel. Once Danya was born, she spent her formative years attending private Jewish schools that taught her that Jesus was a "Jew gone bad" who was trying to drag all the good little Jewish children down to hell.

Danya worked for an alternative radio station in our town that boasted the highest rated morning drive time audience. Danya was the weather and traffic girl and sidekick to a shock jock named Frank.[6] In an ironic twist, it turns out that Frank is the son of a Nazarene pastor. During their Monday morning on-air banter, Frank often asked Danya what she did over the weekend. The Monday after Danya first visited our church, she surprised everyone by declaring, "I went to church!" Frank replied, "Church? You are not a church kind of person." Danya told Frank, "I know. But I'm learning that Jesus has some interesting things to say about life."

As the weeks went on, members of our church listened on their Monday commutes as Danya updated Frank on her spiritual journey. For Danya, Jesus was no longer the "Jew gone bad," but someone whose life and teachings were captivating. There was something to this Jesus, but she couldn't put her finger on it just yet.

Danya had a lot of questions for our community: questions about Jesus' life; questions about how Jesus viewed the Old Testament Law; questions about grace; questions about being kosher; and questions about why Christians had abandoned the Jewish festivals. After many conversations, reading books and countless cups of Starbucks coffee, Danya began to see Jesus in a different light.

All of Danya's questions weren't answered perfectly, but one Sunday afternoon Danya was lying on her bed, thinking about the spiritual journey she had been on. Suddenly, she felt overwhelmed by a presence. She said, "It felt like hands were holding me up and supporting me. I can't explain it other than I was overcome with emotion and knew that I was loved by a gracious Messiah who would never let me go." Danya invited Jesus to be her Messiah and announced on "The Frank Show" the next morning that she was now a follower of Jesus. A couple weeks later, through tears and sobs, Danya blubbered through her story to our community and was baptized in one of our member's swimming pools.

Sometimes people like Danya come to faith because they are in full pursuit of truth, meaning, and beauty. In these cases, our job is to be kind, spiritual coaches and mentors, helping them think through their journey. But by far, the most common type of spiritual conversations I have with people revolve around coming to grips with the spiritual baggage of the past.

The Baggage of Religion

I first met Kacy at the concert of a mutual friend. It may have been due to the number of drinks that Kacy had, but when she found out I was a pastor, she shared an unsolicited description of her spiritual past. It turned out that Kacy grew up in a house church in a small town. The small house church was very exclusive. In fact, they believed their small movement was the only group that was going to make it to heaven. Kacy's childhood was full of rigid and legalistic practices.

When Kacy hit her late teen years, she began to wonder about her family's church. She had a lot of questions for the leaders of her church, but questions were strongly discouraged in their sect. At some point shortly after high school, the cognitive dissonance of her life became overwhelming. If her church was so amazing, she wondered, why did it make people worse human beings and not better people? Not knowing any other alternatives, she left the only faith that she knew and gave up on Jesus.

As the years went by, there was a nagging in Kacy's soul. She realized a lot of the religious baggage from her childhood church had nothing to do with Jesus. She also knew that underneath all that baggage there was something real. There was something undeniable that she couldn't live without.

So in a noisy concert hall late one Friday night, Kacy spoke over the music and asked me, "How can you separate those things? How do you get around the baggage of religion to what is really real?" I didn't know how to give her a short answer, so I said, "Come and do life with our community of faith." To my surprise, she did.

Kacy has been at our church for a few months now, interacting with the people of our community. She even joined a small group for the first time. A couple weeks ago, I asked her how she was doing on her spiritual journey. Kacy's eyes began to well up and after a long pause she said, "When I am able to get some words out, I will try and tell you."

More than anything, people like Kacy need to see examples of a healthy community. They need to see firsthand the power of the local church. Bill Hybels, the founding pastor of Willow Creek Community Church, is fond of saying, "There is nothing like the church when it is working right."[7] But I would add a corollary to that axiom: "There is nothing more messed up than the church when it is dysfunctional."

Ironically, to be effective at evangelism in a postindividualistic era, we need to focus less on old formulas and sales pitches of evangelism methodologies of the past and more on understanding people as individuals. What drives a person to a personal encounter with Jesus is different for every person. What all of these experiences have in common is this: a person may learn something about Christian truth-claims through a sermon or a book, but the beauty and goodness of the Christian faith can only be evaluated and experienced through a relationship with what Lewis Rambo calls an "advocate."[8] For thousands of years now, God's revelation comes through real people embodying the love, grace, and beauty of God. The gospel can change the world. As Jesus modeled, this happens through the transformation of human beings through a personal encounter. The word for that is evangelism.

Discussion Questions

1. What happens when the Abrahamic blessing gets imbalanced? How have you seen this happen in your own experience?

2. How does evangelism remain a very important enterprise in the missional church?

3. If you came to faith as an adult, which category of evangelism best represented your experience: personal crisis, persistent love, spiritual quest, or religious baggage?

4. Have you ever given in to the American temptation to see results too quickly in someone's life? Explain.

5. Why is it important to focus on the uniqueness of an individual's journey when it comes to evangelism?

Recommended Readings

Crandall, Ron. *The Contagious Witness*. Nashville: Abingdon, 1999.

Guder, Darrell L., et al. *Missional Church: A Vision for the Sending Church in North America*. Grand Rapids: Eerdmans, 1998.

Hybels, Bill. *Just Walk Across the Room*. Grand Rapids: Zondervan, 2006.

McLaren, Brian. *More Ready than You Realize: Evangelism as a Dance in the Postmodern Matrix*. Grand Rapids: Zondervan, 2002.

Stone, Bryan. *Evangelism after Christendom: The Theology and Practice of Christian Witness*. Grand Rapids: Brazos Press, 2007.

About the Author

Dr. Dana Hicks (Asbury Theological Seminary) is the lead pastor of Real Life Community Church of the Nazarene in Nampa, Idaho, and an adjunct professor of Missional Leadership at Northwest Nazarene University. Previously he was the founding pastor of Beginnings Church of the Nazarene in Tucson, Arizona, and the lead pastor of Grays Harbor Church of the Nazarene in Hoquiam, Washington.

4

MISSIONAL GENERATIVE LEADERSHIP

Gerhard Weigelt and Morris Weigelt
Mason, Michigan

GERHARD AND MORRIS WEIGELT are privileged to serve God together. This son and his father serve on a ministry team in small-town America in a church with a long history of effective ministry in their community. Mason First Church of the Nazarene was founded by E. W. Martin, whose motto for ministry was "Respect for the Past, Progress for the Present, and Vision for the Future." Together, the Weigelts continue to move forward, seeking God's vision for the future of their congregation. Learn from this multigenerational ministry team as they seek God's best for their local church, believing that multigenerational leadership will provide the environment in which God can build his church.

THE CHALLENGE: THE CONTEXT

Mason, Michigan, is a small county seat town of 8,200 people located in central Michigan just south of Lansing, the state's capital city. The town is surrounded by farmland and, at the same time, sits in the shadow of Michigan State University with all of its resources.

The church originated in a revival meeting sponsored by the teens of Lansing First Church of the Nazarene back in the 1930s. The street meetings soon progressed into cottage prayer meetings, and then into storefronts over the first several years. In 1931, the church was organized and the congregation soon purchased and converted the local dance hall into their place of worship. In the late 1950s the congregation built the church's present facility on land donated by a church member. Moving forward with a missional vision, our congregation voted in 1998 to purchase a forty-five-acre parcel of land to help them continue to reach out to the needs of our community. After many years of praying, planning, and sacrificing, we just completed the construction of our ROC, or Recreational Outreach Center—a community center serving the spiritual needs of Mason and its surrounding communities.

Mason First Church has been blessed over the years with godly leaders with a great vision for the future. Pastor Gerhard observes, "We now find ourselves with a unique pastoral team." Gerhard is blessed to serve as the lead pastor of this fine congregation. Until roughly two years ago, Gerhard served at Mason First as an associate pastor under the visionary leadership of Mark D. Rigg. Today, he leads a multigenerational ministry team. The church's youth minister, who is in his early thirties, focuses on the spiritual growth of teenagers and their families; the children's pastor is in his early forties and guides the spiritual development of children and their families; and Pastor Gerhard's father, Dr. Morris A. Weigelt—now in his late seventies, serves as teacher in residence, chaplain to the staff, and research consultant for staff members. "I believe the multigenerational aspect of this ministry team provides some wonderful opportunities for generating vision and growth and congregational mission," Gerhard remarks.

THE VISION: MISSIONAL DISCIPLESHIP

When Mason First Church's last pastoral transition began, the ministry staff and church board leadership were studying *Simple Church* and *Transformational Church*, both authored by Thom Rainer, with his colleagues Eric Geiger and Ed Stetzer, respectively. The challenge of guiding the congregation into a fruitful missional future led Mason First's ministry team to seek God's face together, asking God to guide them toward the congregation's next steps of obedience.

Soon after my election as lead pastor, the staff participated in a retreat to visualize and strategize our future. In that vital retreat our multigenerational staff came to a clear focus on relational transformation and captured it in the tagline: "Together Seeking and Celebrating Transforming Relationships."

We believe that God is calling us as a church family together to seek and celebrate transforming relationships. Why is he calling us to this? Because transformation is central to the message of Jesus Christ! God sent his Son Jesus Christ to earth to repair the damage that sin has caused in our world, to restore relationships, and to transform lives. The purpose of our investment in the kingdom of God is transformed lives—lives in which the damage of sin has been reversed and the image of God is restored.

Stetzer and Rainer designate transformation as a nonnegotiable for the church "because radical change is the heart of the Christian message and because the power of the gospel changes everything—lives, churches, and communities."[1] Paul's vision of the church in 2 Corinthians 3:18 describes that radical change: "And we all, who with unveiled faces contemplate the Lord's glory, are being transformed into his image with ever-increasing glory, which comes from the Lord, who is the Spirit." My father observed: "If transformation is not occurring, it is deceptive—even flat wrong, to call it church." Christ died for more than a superficial change: only a radical transformation will do.

THE IMPLEMENTATION: GENERATIVITY THROUGH MULTIGENERATIONAL LEADERSHIP

It has been fascinating to see the ways in which God is using our multigenerational staff to guide lifelong spiritual formation in this congregation in a small Michigan town. The patterns and values of this multifaceted ministry, as we understand them, are as follows.

Patterns of a Multigenerational Leadership Team

In light of the congregation's vision of "Together Seeking and Celebrating Transforming Relationships," our pastoral staff functions as a team. Staff meetings and periodic planning retreats involve each person with full rights and privileges. Celebrations of God's work among us and within our entire congregation are part of these meetings. We carefully nurture the relationships we enjoy together and offer each other accountability and prayer and unconditional love. The interchange of ideas within the staff context is free and stimulating. We carefully discuss programs in each of our specific areas of responsibility for purposes of close interaction.

In order to keep growing together, the staff reads and discusses significant books together at staff meetings. We are currently working our way through Marva Dawn's *The Sense of the Call: A Sabbath Way of Life for Those Who Serve God, the Church, and the World*, in which she notes that "the sense of our call is that God's Kingdom reclaims us, revitalizes us, and renews us and thus reigns through us before others, on behalf of others, sometimes in spite of others, and always with others."[2] We have also explored other books, including Eugene Peterson's *Christ Plays in Ten Thousand Places*[3] and *Making Disciples: One Conversation at a Time* by D. Michael Henderson.[4]

The staff shares platform responsibilities, planning duties, and offering leadership to worship. Tag-team sermons are preached with some regularity, involving two-person and three-person combinations. During a recent sermon on prayer by our lead pastor, congregants were invited to text their primary concerns and insights about prayer to the youth pastor during the service. After cataloging the issues we received, on another Sunday we—as a pastoral staff—responded to their issues with a member of our congregation—a local prosecuting attorney—as the facilitator. Several times we have chosen a significant biblical text and three different people have preached on that text on successive Sundays. Our Easter service included three pastors focusing on the preresurrection anxiety of Simon Peter, Mary, and John—and the way the resurrection of our Lord offered specialized and specific release to the full investment in kingdom ministry.

The staff shares a common concern for lifelong spiritual formation in our congregation. We are not satisfied with merely presenting a valuable worship experience each week and permitting people to stagnate spiritually. We intentionally create contexts in which the whole family is involved in ongoing spiritual formation. We invite people in our congregation to teach elective courses that build relationships and grow stronger, maturing Christians. Transformation really is the name of the game for us. Recognizing the nature and significance of Christian maturation through resources like James W. Fowler's *Stages of Faith*,[5] the congregation's overall design for personal and spiritual growth is made personal. We agree with Reggie McNeal when he writes, "I don't think the answer is to raise the bar for church members in terms of institutional support. I think the solution is an abandonment of the church culture idolatry and a radical reintroduction of spiritual formation."[6] We are convinced that multigenerational leadership facilitates that goal.

The leadership team at Mason First clearly understands the role of Scripture in spiritual formation. "Christians believe that Scripture provides inspiration and guidance in Christian faith and practice. The Bible does more than inform; it also forms and transforms."[7] The staff guides and designs ministries that highlight the power and authority of Scripture in our people while building transforming relationships. We have been using programs such as "Engage the Word," "Illuminate,"[8] and "One Month to Live"[9] to invite our congregants to live in the same Bible passages and grow together. During the "Engage the Word" series, our children's pastor created illustrated daily devotionals for the children as well. During Lent we used the scriptures found in the Book of Common Prayer as our central focus. Daily devotions were written by eighty-five different members of our congregation and were distributed via daily emails. The overall topic was Lenten obedience and Easter joy. As both a leadership team and congregation, our mutual accountability of wrestling with assigned lectionary texts together has been particularly enriching.

As Mason First Church's teacher in residence, Dr. Morris Weigelt serves as an invaluable resource person to the entire staff. His wealth of experience as emeritus professor of New Testament and spiritual formation at Nazarene Theological Seminary offers depths of insight to exegetical questions and bibliographical needs. He leads the staff discussions of their current book under study and offers broad research in support of his fellow ministry team members. The lead pastor and the teacher in residence each have a Kindle on the same account, enabling the teacher in residence to highlight significant material so the lead pastor can read more efficiently.

Values of Multigenerational Leadership

Multigenerational leadership gives the church the energy and passion of youth with the wisdom and experience of the more seasoned leader.

This enables us to discuss issues and avoid some of the impulsive overreactions and the pitfalls of rash, uninformed statements.

Multigenerational leadership provides team accountability and support as we pray both together and for each other in the process of a unified vision for congregational missional discipleship. This vision is colored and guided by the variety of viewpoints and the complementary range of education and preparation for our assignments to specific segments of the congregation. Even though two of our staff members attended the same undergraduate institution, our choice of majors within that university provides enriching variety. Study of the patterns of spiritual development of the age-groups for which each is responsible makes it possible for help in guiding individuals, families, and groups in a far more efficient way.

Multigenerational leadership offers the privilege of multiple voices and viewpoints in making major decisions. Our periodic planning retreats are enriched by the giftedness of the viewpoints and backgrounds of each member of the team. None of us will soon forget the planning session in which our current vision came into focus: "Together Seeking and Celebrating Transforming Relationships." The sense of joy and awareness of the Spirit's guidance were apparent to us all, which has since led us to refer to our new ROC community center as a "Relational Opportunity Center."

Multigenerational leadership offers our congregation a variety of voices in worship leadership and proclamation of the motivating vision of missional discipleship. To hear this central passion articulated by various people who are aware of our congregation's broad needs enriches everyone and leads us to trust the credibility of the entire team.

Multigenerational leadership presents the gospel to the congregation with different styles and emphases. Each of our staff members offers a unique communication style. Tag-team sermons take full advantage of these styles and, in the process, reach a wider variety of needs and ages within our congregation. As our pastors focus on different segments in our specialized congregational assignments, we are provided new understandings of the needs and preferred methods of comprehension and enriched communication with the congregation. The choice of illustrations and the use of various forms of media keep the interest and attention of our congregants and eliminate the potential boredom of a single voice and viewpoint.

Multigenerational leadership enables the choice and employment of the volunteers in the various ministries. Each person has relationships with others on a level of acquaintance with their skills, passion, and giftedness. Sharing that information at the staff level offers the option of helping volunteers find the area that best fits their unique gift mix.

Multigenerational leadership provides the opportunity to have age-specific counseling for our congregants. The lead pastor, of course, carries the heaviest load in this area but is free to discuss methodology and direction from the staff member most directly involved.

Multigenerational leadership deepens the spiritual formation of the congregation at several levels. Our interaction with each other as a team brings growth and accountability to each of us. Our guidance of volunteers allows us to mentor them in their individual spiritual growth. Our contacts with those in our areas of specific responsibility enable us as a team to be in close contact with a wider range of people than would be possible for a single pastor. Information shared with each other at staff meetings alerts us to the needs of congregants that might well be overlooked or unrecognized by a single pastor.

Multigenerational leadership alerts the whole team to "touchy" issues and disgruntled people before the situation grows into a major confrontation. We are able to protect and inform and guide each other in multiple ways.

Multigenerational leadership offers a context in which spiritual development for various age-levels is modeled by the members of the staff. Intergenerational spiritual formation is crucial to individual spiritual growth. Awareness of the stages of spiritual formation provides an overview that informs the patterns and program and counseling for a whole range of discipleship. James W. Fowler, in *Stages of Faith: The Psychology of Human Development and the Quest for Meaning*, writes about "the playful seriousness and serious playfulness" necessary to understand and guide the movements of transformation, the unique features, and the predictable stages of faith development.[10] That same awareness enables the members of the team to speak the "language" of each of the groups for which they are responsible—and, in the process, teach each other better ways to communicate vision and content across the full spectrum of the congregation. We subscribe to the definition of spiritual formation by Mark Maddix: "A definition of Christian spiritual formation emphasizes it as a lifelong process that takes place in the context of community."[11]

Multigenerational leadership not only provides an awareness of developmental stages but also offers the opportunity to model those stages by current leaders. Understanding the "architecture" of spiritual formation, transformation, and discipleship demands a greater awareness of the entire life journey. At Mason First Church we are working together to articulate and implement spiritual formation and missional discipleship from the cradle to the grave. Richard Rohr in *Falling Upward*[12] differentiates between the formational tasks in the first half of our spiritual lives and the last half of life and urges us to become mature Christians in the broadest sense of the term. The search for theological balance, both biblically and experientially, is enriched and facilitated by the range of ages in the leadership team.

Multigenerational leadership provides a setting in which "generativity" in the spiritual formation sense, in the employment of congregational leadership sense, and in the long-term congregational development sense will outlast the current leadership team. We believe that God wants to do a long-range work among us that will continue to have ripples long after this team of leaders is gone—in fact, until Jesus returns and the kingdom reaches full fruition. We long to help our congregation "lean into God's promised future for us and for all being . . . to be part of the reconciling, redeeming and restoring work that goes on wherever the Kingdom of God is breaking in."[13]

Multigenerational leadership augments and enriches authentic long-term generativity in spiritual formation—at the individual and the congregational and community levels too. To God be the glory!

Discussion Questions

1. How is a cradle-to-the-grave pattern of spiritual formation formulated and implemented at the congregational level given the unique character of your people?

2. How is it possible to enhance generativity in spiritual formation through gathering data and opinions from all age ranges customized to meet the needs of your particular congregation?

3. What are the values of multigenerational leadership for immediate and long-range leadership in spiritual formation at the congregational level in the setting in which you minister? For immediate and long-range decision making at the congregational level?

4. How does multigenerational leadership contribute to communication at the congregational level given the structure and makeup of your specific setting?

Recommended Readings

Leclerc, Diane, and Mark A. Maddix, eds. *Spiritual Formation: A Wesleyan Paradigm*. Kansas City: Beacon Hill Press of Kansas City, 2011.

Rainer, Thom S., and Eric Geiger. *Simple Church: Returning to God's Process for Making Disciples*. Nashville: Broadman and Holman, 2006.

Rohr, Richard. *Falling Upward: A Spirituality for the Two Halves of Life*. San Francisco: John Wiley and Sons, 2011.

Stetzer, Ed, and Thom S. Rainer. *Transformational Church: Creating a New Scorecard for Congregations*. Nashville: Broadman and Holman, 2010.

Tracy, Wesley D., E. Dee Freeborn, Janine Tartaglia, and Morris A. Weigelt. *The Upward Call: Spiritual Formation and the Holy Life*. Kansas City: Beacon Hill Press of Kansas City, 1994.

About the Authors

Rev. Gerhard F. Weigelt graduated from MidAmerica Nazarene University in 1993 and Nazarene Theological Seminary in 1997. He joined the pastoral staff at Mason First Church of the Nazarene as an associate in August of 1997 and was elected lead pastor in December of 2010.

Dr. Morris A. Weigelt is currently teacher in residence at Mason, Michigan, First Church of the Nazarene. He pastored in Connecticut, taught for a decade in the religion department at Northwest Nazarene College, and then taught for three decades at Nazarene Theological Seminary in the areas of New Testament studies and spiritual formation. He is one of the authors of *The Upward Call: Spiritual Formation and the Holy Life* and of *Living the Lord's Prayer: The Heart of Spiritual Formation.*

5

ENGAGING
GOD'S MISSION
IN AND FOR COMMUNITIES

Ryan Pugh
Portland, Oregon

NOT LONG AGO, I had the opportunity of leading over three hundred fifty high school students and staff at a summer camp in Idaho's beautiful mountains. For five days we journeyed together in reimagining our lives around the kingdom of God that was ushered into this world through the life, death, and resurrection of Jesus of Nazareth. We reimagined our lives around Jesus' kingdom virtue of love and what it might look like to love God with our entire selves and to love others as we love ourselves. We reimagined a world built around treating all people in light of the beautiful image of God in which they were created. We reimagined our lives around the justice of God, which seeks actively to restore the world to the way God created it to be. We reimagined a world of people who follow Jesus in a race to the bottom instead of the top, humbly serving the least, the last, and the lost. And we reimagined a world founded on the love and relationship found in community rather than our cultural bent toward hyper-individualism. To put it simply, we reimagined what it means to throw ourselves headlong into God's kingdom and mission of restoring the world to its intended wholeness.

I invite you to do some of your own reimagining as you read this chapter. In the following pages, I hope you will be drawn into reimagining with me what it might look like for local bodies of Christ followers to engage God's mission in and for the communities in which they live. Through stories and thoughts, you will be guided in reimagining the action and role of the church in the world. In the end, I hope that the same restoring God who "moved into the neighborhood" (John 1:14, TM) will capture your heart and life, empowering you to be that same kind of presence in your local community.

Before diving into some creative ways that local churches might engage God's mission in their communities, we need to understand that God's mission is the restoration of all creation to its beautiful, intended wholeness. While God's good creation is broken and wounded, God continues to work through God's people, toward the end of all creation being made new (Rev. 21:1-5). Engaging this mission of God, through holy and righteous living, is the ultimate call upon our lives. As Chris Folmsbee notes, "Each of us has been created in God's image in order to remind the broken world that God has not forgotten it and to participate with God in his mission to unbreak the world."[1]

Perhaps the most significant lesson to grasp about this mission is that it is just that: *God's* mission. We are not called to bring our mission into our local context. We are called to enter into partnership with God in what God is already doing in the lives of people in our communities. As Brad Brisco indicates, "We often wrongly assume that the primary activity of God is in the church, rather than recognizing that God's primary activity is in the world, and the church is God's instrument sent into the world to participate in his redemptive mission."[2] God's mission is ours, and all throughout Scripture, God's people are sent into the world in order to join God in this mission. This sending of God's people to join God's mission is most apparent in John's account of the gospel. In John 20:21, John writes, "As the Father has sent me, I am sending you." Referring to this verse, John Stott remarks that the mission of the church is explicitly articulated in the Fourth Gospel:

> The crucial form in which the Great Commission has been handed down to us (though it is the most neglected because it is the most costly) is the Johannine. Jesus had anticipated it in his prayer in the upper room, which he said to the Father: "As thou didst send me into the world, so I have sent them into the world" (John 17:18). Now, probably in the same upper room but after his death and resurrection, he turned his prayer-statement into a commission and said: "As the Father has sent me, even so I send you" (John 20:21). In both these sentences Jesus did more than draw a vague parallel between his mission and ours. Deliberately and precisely he made his mission the *model* of ours, saying "*as* the Father has sent me, even *so* I send you." Therefore our understanding of the church's mission must be deduced from our understanding of the Son's.[3]

The church knows her mission when she knows the mission of Jesus. Jürgen Moltmann put it another way: "It is not the church that has a mission of salvation to fulfill in the world; it is the mission of the Son and the Spirit through the Father that includes the church."[4]

When we understand and confess that we are called to join God's mission in the world, the reimagining of how we might "do church" is underway. Instead of focusing our energies on getting people to our churches through programs, budgets, and buildings, we're freed to move the church outside our four walls and find God in the world.

Understanding that God is already at work in the world and that God's primary action is in the world should lead churches to two things. First, as churches recognize that God's action is in the world, they should be drawn to listen to the stories and needs of others in the community before diving in. Jon Huckins and Rob Yackley write, "As a missional community seeking to engage our local contexts with the good news of Jesus, we choose to view our neighborhoods and our cities as classrooms. If we are to be good news, we need to listen to the needs and dreams of our surrounding contexts."[5] If we fail to listen, we run the very real risk of placing our own agendas upon the community, rather than seeking to discover what God is already doing in our midst.

When churches adopt a listening posture, they follow Jesus' lead since listening requires humility and an attitude of service. In his book *Equip*, Tim Milburn invents a new term that captures Jesus' life of submission to God's will and devotion to God's mission: the word is "submissional."[6] Throughout his life, Jesus' posture of listening and servanthood demonstrates his submission to the will of the Father, emptying himself and becoming a servant (Phil. 2). This submission is for a purpose, namely that of participating in God's mission of redemption, reconciliation, and restoration. To be submissional is to be concerned with what God is doing in the world and in what God is calling us to participate.[7]

When churches listen first to their communities, tangible opportunities for engagement with other people and organizations become evident.

Because we recognize God's prevenient action, working with others in the community can become our most passionate desire. As we connect with others with similar values, churches can extend their impact. For instance, if a church desires to develop relationships with homeless people in their community, that congregation can partner with an organization with the same desire, whether or not the organization claims Christ.

Likewise, churches with a vision to help families with students who struggle in school could work with a local after-school tutoring program, perhaps even offering their congregation's facilities to be used for student work—or even launching a new program if one doesn't already exist. Or a church in a community of low-income families could invite their neighbors to join them in starting a sustainable garden that offers healthy food and nutrition.

The community of Christ followers at Castle Hills Church of the Nazarene in Boise, Idaho, chose to do just that in the summer of 2012. By venturing outside its walls and beginning a community garden with a simple purpose of providing "fresh, healthy produce to those in the neighboring communities who might otherwise go without," a half acre of rocky land sitting next to the church's grassy baseball field and dog park became the perfect spot to dig, plant, tend, and harvest. But a different kind of "harvest" came up before anything was even planted: over ten tons of rock were hand-picked by the community from this potential life-giving plot of garden land! The aptly named Solid Rock Community Garden is now a place of life-sustaining food and life-giving relationships.

As the community garden at Castle Hills began to take shape, more than fifty community service workers joined church members for their first garden workday in November 2010. Together they dug rocks, moved soil, and spread leaves for pending winter months. What started as one person's desire to focus less on himself and more on others has turned into a community-wide partnership of restoration. Since that time, many conversations about faith, beauty, hurt, pain, doubt, and sorrow have taken place in and around the garden, and many more conversations were had at the church's first harvest celebration. Community service workers and their families shared a meal with the people of Castle Hills, enjoying each other's stories about how produce from the garden has impacted individuals, families, food banks, shelters, and even a local cafe. God has been at work in the Solid Rock Community Garden at Castle Hills because of one congregation's willingness to engage God's mission in a creative way. When churches are open to what God is already doing in the community around them, countless missional opportunities arise.

It is important to note here that the success of the Solid Rock Community Garden or other creative ministries like the ones mentioned here in engaging God's mission is not dependent on a logical "return on investment." As we evaluate what we are doing, we must also recognize that God's action is often very inefficient, or even seemingly reckless. As Jesus teaches in Luke 15, God's amazing grace is like a woman who loses a coin and then spends a fortune celebrating its recovery; or a shepherd who abandons ninety-nine sheep in the wilderness to search for one lost lamb; or an aging Middle Eastern father whose wayward son has abandoned him, only to focus his sights on the horizons of his estate, longing for the boy's return. As we participate in God's action, our calling is to be faithful, even if some might deem our efforts unsuccessful. Creative ministries like a community garden, whose overall purpose is to engage God's mission in and for the community, are not to be a means to a greater end. As we focus on creating relationships with others, our efforts should not be intended to merely influence people. Let's face it: it doesn't feel too good to be someone's "mission." Yet that's often the way we seem to view our role as Christians in the world: to form relationships with "non-Christians" in order to influence them toward a greater goal, like accepting Christ. When a relationship is formed and shaped by a dominant party influencing the other, it cannot be a true relationship. In such cases, one party views the other as an object that can be controlled and can opt out at any time the influence isn't working. Instead, real relationships are founded on the reality of the incarnate Christ found in two people sharing life together, encountering Christ as they share joy, pain, and the fullness of human life. Andrew Root, professor of youth and family ministries at Luther Seminary, writes,

> Ministry, then, is not about "using" relationships to get individuals to accept a "third thing," whether that is conservative politics, moral behaviors, or even the gospel message. Rather, ministry is about connection, one to another, about sharing in suffering and joy, about persons meeting persons with no pretense or secret motives. It is about shared life, confessing Christ not outside the relationships but within it.[8]

When partnership ministries are birthed with a desire to serve, to build relationships with others for the sake of the relationship itself, and to encountering Christ together, God's Spirit is freed to work in each person's life. As a result, everyone is invited to be part of what God is doing in and for the community, and new opportunities sprout for the coming of God's kingdom.

Churches that are serious about engaging God's mission of restoring communities to their intended wholeness recognize that being missional actually requires much more than seeing them as elective ministry programs, as valuable as these programs can be. Being a missional church means the life of the congregation revolves around what God is doing in the community. This does not mean that we don't gather corporately, journey in community together, or make disciples, but that these are catalyzed and organized around God's mission in and for the community. Merely adding outreach days or special events to the calendar do not develop missional churches. But when a church is devoted to God's mission, beautiful stories of love and hospitality take place.

A few years ago, a suburban mother of three decided to take seriously Jesus' parable in Matthew 22:1-14 about inviting strangers and outcasts to her party table. As Christmas Day approached, Colleen Norton decided to take action by placing a simple ad on Craigslist that read:

Free Christmas Dinner with New Friends

Are you hitting hard times or lonely and want to have a nice Christmas dinner? Please come and celebrate with my loving family. Please email for my address. Thank you and God bless.[9]

Alan Hirsch and Lance Ford observe that

thirty people responded to Colleen's ad, many wanting to donate food, and six (previously) strangers, including a mother and her two sons, joined Colleen's family for Christmas dinner. One lady said she responded to the ad because her husband was in the hospital recovering from a stroke and she had no one to spend Christmas day with. Colleen said she hopes to teach her three daughters the importance of helping others and that Christmas is about reaching out to others. "I like to believe that my girls learn that they're really blessed in life," she said. "If we were hitting hard times, we would hope that someone would be there for us."

Colleen simply considered her resources, made herself available, and stepped out of the ordinary into the extraordinary. She ignored her limitations and considered what she could do over and above what she could not do.[10]

A church full of Colleens—set on God's mission of offering hope, joy, and peace to the world—can change a community, as well as the world. Many people are hungry for a church that is willing to reimagine its role in its local community. Others are desperate for a church that listens to the community and world around them, seeking to engage God where God is already working and joining forces with others in order to see God restore communities to their intended wholeness. As we are willing to reimagine what it looks like to engage God's mission, I am hopeful that we can find new life and new opportunities, in our own lives and in the life of our communities.

So go ahead, think outside the walls, and reimagine what God would have you do in your community. It might not only change your community but could change you as well.

Discussion Questions

1. What changes when we grasp that the mission we are called to live into is God's mission?

2. Consider Jürgen Moltmann's statement again: "It is not the church that has a mission of salvation to fulfill in the world; it is the mission of the Son and the Spirit through the Father that includes the church." What is the significance of confessing that the mission is God's and the church is included in it?

3. What do you think of the claim that a relationship built on one party influencing the other is not a true relationship? What might this mean for you, your church, and your creative missional ministries to focus on genuine, no-agenda relationships?

4. What are some obstacles that churches face in getting outside of their buildings to become actively involved in their communities?

5. What is God already doing in your community? How might you join in? How can you listen better for where God is at work? What people and/or organizations could you partner with in order to serve?

Recommended Readings

Ford, Lance, and Brad Brisco. *Missional Essentials: A Guide for Experiencing God's Mission in Your Life.* Kansas City: House Studio, 2012.

Huckins, Jon, and Rob Yackley. *Thin Places: 6 Postures for Creating and Practicing Missional Community.* Kansas City: House Studio, 2012.

O'Connor, Elizabeth. *Call to Commitment.* New York: Harper and Row, 1975.

Vanier, Jean. *Community and Growth.* Mahwah, NJ: Paulist Press, 1989.

About the Author

As a member of the Community of Adsideo in Portland, Oregon, Ryan Pugh is seeking to join God in the restoration of the city and its people. Ryan is passionate about the church being the living presence of Christ in the world. He is the author of *The Money Experiment: A Community Practice in Financial Simplicity* (House Studio, 2012). Ryan enjoys reading, writing, basketball, and hanging out with friends and the community around him.

6

MISSIONAL COMMUNITIES

Mark A. Maddix
Northwest Nazarene University

INTRODUCTION

As we have seen, one of the growing developments in the missional church movement is the focus on community in general and more particularly, on the local church being part of a larger missional community. Many younger missional disciples today wrestle with their place in the local church, choosing instead to engage more directly in culture to fulfill God's mission in the world.

However, one of the strong benchmarks of missional discipleship is the need for a community of believers who trust in God and depend on each other. This runs counter to the individualistic bent so common in Western society today. Missional disciples participate in a form of Christian community that recognizes the value of being composed of many members from diverse backgrounds and narratives.

LED BY THE HOLY SPIRIT

The purpose of missional communities is to represent the compassion, justice, and reign of God on earth. The distinct aspect of missional communities is that they are shaped by the power of the Holy Spirit who creates, guides, and sustains God's people. Missional communities are not empowered merely by human activity alone, but by God's empowering presence. Through the power of the Holy Spirit, a sent people are cultivated through practices by which they are formed and shaped as missional disciples. The primary difference in developing missional communities is that the Spirit is not identified as working in individuals only but primarily through community. Christian community functions primarily through the work of the Spirit in community as disciples discern God's leading through Scripture, tradition, reason, and experience. It is through the community that the Spirit is active by gathering, empowering, and sending God's people to be engaged in mission.

It is through missional communities that believers engage in God's redemption of humanity and creation. Missional disciples today, like the earliest generations of Christ followers, believe the Spirit is an eschatological reality that represents the fullness of God's creative purpose. While this orientation was indicated by Jesus' announcement of the reign of God, the early church spoke of the reality of God's reign in terms of the dynamic presence of the Holy Spirit. Both were declaring that God's future salvation—the reconciliation of all humanity and the healing of all creation—had become a present reality.[1] Missional disciples find themselves between the reality of the final consummation of Christ's reign and the power of the present reality of God's restoration and healing of all of creation. This in-between time of the "already" and "not yet" kingdom of God means the kingdom is here "already" as the power of God in Jesus Christ through the Spirit at work all around us. But it is also "not yet" in that it will only be when Jesus returns that the kingdom will be established fully. The "already" means all the kingdom that will be fully realized when Jesus returns is partially realized now. The work of God we see in the world today is just a foretaste of what we will see when Jesus returns.

Missional communities recognize what God is doing in the context of the community as missional disciples are being formed, shaped, and sent into the world by participating in what God is doing in the world. In many ways, missional communities are hermeneutical bodies that discern what God is doing as they participate in the reign of God on earth. The reign of God on earth takes place as people engage in acts of compassion and mercy.

PRACTICES OF MISSIONAL COMMUNITIES

Missional communities that embrace the work of the Holy Spirit in community live according to a variety of Christian practices. Not all missional communities are the same, since the imaginative work of the Holy Spirit is far-reaching. However, missional communities differ sharply from traditional church practice. In broad terms, traditional churches provide activities and programs that seek to sustain the life of the congregation. The activities foster attendance, giving, and serving in the church. Missional communities are primarily concerned with maturation and growth centered on following the life of Jesus. These communities are often more organic and less programmatic and focus on the interconnectivity of communal practice and personal formation. Such practices as hospitality, generosity, service, transparency, compassion, and grace are necessary to build and sustain community. Leslie Newbigin has identified six practices of missional communities:

1. They practice corporate praise, thanksgiving, gratitude, and grace.
2. They declare truth that challenges the reigning plausibility structures.
3. They establish relationship within a local neighborhood.
4. They encourage mutual service in the priesthood of all believers.
5. They expect mutual responsibility rather than individualism.
6. They nurture hope and reimagine a vision of the future.[2]

Newbigin's list provides a basis for a broader discussion about practices of missional communities. Newbigin's practices provide a framework to explore and develop missional communities. All of these practices are not explored here, but some of these practices are included in the following discussion about how missional communities are developed and sustained. These practices include worship, *koinonia*, the priesthood of all believers, and local community engagement.

MISSION BEGINS IN WORSHIP

Missional disciples are sent into the world to participate in God's redemption. Before they can be sent into the world, God's mission begins *within* the church, the body of Christ. As Christians gather in worship around both the word and the table, God's healing mission begins. The relationships that are shared in community provide a witness to others of God's grace. As Christians practice acceptance, love, and hospitality they witness to God's healing mission. The church is a witness to the world of God's love, grace, and compassion. As the church engages in the world, missional disciples provide God's healing in the world, centered in love.

The church becomes the place where the narrative of God is lived and mission is practiced in the real world. Missional communities begin by recognizing that mission first begins *within* the church before the church can be God's witnesses to the world. As the church encounters the renewing love of God in the communal worship of Scripture, prayers, offering, and the Eucharist, it is transformed to proclaim hope and forgiveness to be God's flesh and blood to the world. The church's participation in God's mission during the week continues through communal worship that begins every Lord's Day.

KOINONIA

Missional communities reflect the practice of the early church. As Luke notes, the earliest Christian generations "devoted themselves to the apostles' teaching and to fellowship, to the breaking of bread and to prayer" (Acts 2:42). The early church recognized the communal reality of holy living, mutual support, and sacrificial service that is expressed in the New Testament view of *koinonia*. A missional community combats the current cultural norms of independence, self-interest, and privatized faith for an order of interdependence, shared responsibility, and mutual instruction. Missional communities are marked by sharing life together through the following avenues:

• Studying and learning
• Sharing meals
• Praying and studying Scripture
• Serving in the community
• Socializing, laughing, and having fun together
• Sharing their story (testimony)
• Offering prayers of healing and encouragement to one another
• Breaking bread and sharing in Communion
• Finding ways to connect with their neighbors through missional engagement

Missional communities possess three distinct traits. First, they place a high view on shared responsibility and mutual accountability. Missional communities follow the example of John Wesley's view that "there is no holiness without social holiness." Wesley's primary intention of "social holiness" was in relation to Christian fellowship, offered as a means of countering privatized notions of Christian faith. Christians cannot grow in God's grace alone but need the support and accountability of other Christians. For Wesley, as Christians participate in the "means of grace" in the context of community, it helps them grow in holiness of heart and life. Wesley's understanding of social holiness led him to organize his "methodical" followers through small groups of societies, classes, and bands. These groups had specific purposes and provided the early Methodists with a framework for spiritual growth in community. Wesley believed that spiritual growth and "holiness of heart and life" required discipline, nurture, and accountability. Wesley's small-group system has similarities to many modern cell groups, support groups, and Bible studies that practice accountability and seek to develop missional disciples.

Second, missional communities value the church's practices as communal. Within the life of the church there are no isolated, private, and individualistic activities. Ecclesial practices involve people in action with one another. It is through the individual's participation in communal life and the church's tradition that a sense of corporate memory is established. Christians are not born knowing how to be missionally engaged in God's redemptive purposes; it is through mentors, teachers, and partners that we are given advice, challenged, and supported to extend and deepen our call to God's mission. These ecclesial practices of worship, prayer, Eucharist, study, and service are experiential and form and shape Christians into missional disciples. These communal practices are reflected in John Wesley's "means of grace." The means of grace are outward signs, words, and actions ordained by God as ordinary channels that convey God's grace. The means of grace provide a taxonomy of practices that help persons grow in Christ-likeness: the Eucharist, Bible reading and proclamation, prayer and fasting, worship, service and social ministry, church and small-group participation. It is through these practices that God conveys his grace toward humanity, thus leading to spiritual maturity and holiness of heart and life.[3]

Third, the development of missional communities is not simply for the benefit of those who participate in Christian community. A community of love rooted in the redemptive reign of God can never be for itself only because God's love is contagious and overflowing. The church not only is for believers but also exists to nurture the social relationships that embody the reconciliation and healing of the world in Jesus Christ. A missional community's sign of success is not found in the number of its members, the quality of its worship, or even the extent of its social engagement. Instead, the success of a missional community is measured by the quality of Christian love experienced in the midst of its communal life and ministry. The value of a missional community is found in its actual involvement and participation in communal practices.[4]

THE PRIESTHOOD OF ALL BELIEVERS

Missional communities are formed and shaped by their leadership. The Spirit empowers the church for mission through the gifts of God's people. Paul speaks of the church's calling in Ephesians 4:11-13: "So Christ himself gave the apostles, the prophets, the evangelists, the pastors and teachers, to equip his people for works of service, so that the body of Christ may be built up until we all reach unity in the faith and in the knowledge of the Son of God and become mature, attaining to the whole measure of the fullness of Christ." The emphasis on the oneness of the body of Christ and the distribution of its gifts is missiological. The church's calling and vocation is given in order to "equip [God's] people for works of service." Paul indicates that certain ministries in the form of individuals (apostles, prophets, evangelists, pastor-teachers) are given to the church by Christ in order for the church to fulfill her task—God's missional purposes in the world. This mission cannot function without the necessary leaders to equip and guide the body in ecclesial practices that shape and form the community of believers to demonstrate God's reign on earth.

Some missional communities argue that the role of the ordained pastor is no longer necessary to "equip and guide" the body of Christ. However, the role of the clergy is to equip, empower, and mobilize the laity. Missional communities cannot be effective with the primary focus on a single pastor or his or her staff members. In missional communities all who are followers of Christ receive the same vocation of mission, and are gifted in various ways for that mission, as they participate in the reign of God. Missional communities move beyond the primary focus of professional, clergy-shaped leadership models to a more decentralized approach that empowers all believers as ministers. This does not negate the importance of ordained clergy, but it redefines the role of clergy as servant leaders who embody the mutual contribution of the "priesthood of believers." The New Testament affirms the priesthood of the Christian community as a whole. Believers are "being built into a spiritual house to be a holy priesthood, offering spiritual sacrifices acceptable to God through Jesus Christ" (1 Pet. 2:5; see Rom. 12:1; Heb. 13:15-16). Therefore, the central idea of priesthood applies to the people of God. As a priesthood, the *whole* church has the privilege of access to God (Heb. 4:16).[5]

Since missional communities value living and serving in community, missional leaders focus their time, energy, and thinking on the formation of a covenant community. This covenant community includes mutual accountability, participation in ecclesial practices, and leading people in spiritual disciplines to enable them to participate in God's mission. Also, the missional leader recognizes the importance of vocation and "calling," not only to traditional forms of ministry but in all aspects of vocational life. Since there is no separation between the sacred and the secular, and God is at work in the world, Christians view their vocation of being a teacher, lawyer, carpenter, businessperson, salesperson, politician, and so forth, as their vocational "calling." As they engage in their vocations, they are making the kingdom of God present. They do not view these professions merely as "jobs" but as God's calling. Missional leaders uphold the "priesthood of believers" by empowering Christians to see their vocations as God's calling to enable them to engage in God's mission in the world. When Lesslie Newbigin was asked, what kind of leadership will nourish the church in faithful witness to the gospel in a pluralist society? He answered by saying that the task of leadership is "to lead the congregation as a whole in a mission to the community as a whole, to claim its whole public life, as well as the lives of all its people, for God's rule."[6] This is the kind of missional leadership that is needed to form and sustain missional communities in a changing world and culture.

LOCAL COMMUNITY ENGAGEMENT

Many traditional churches give primary focus to overseas missions. These experiences provide transformation and growth for those who engage in service to others. These global mission experiences provide both the participant and the recipient the opportunity to complete a specific project or ministry objective. Even though these experiences are valuable, missional communities recognize that the primary role of the church is to engage in contextualized mission—in their local neighborhood. Missional engagement is not something that is global but local—"glocal."

When Jesus was asked by the Sadducees about which is the greatest commandment, Jesus answered by saying, "'Love the Lord your God with all your heart and with all your soul and with all your mind.' This is the first and greatest commandment. And the second is like it: 'Love your neighbor as yourself.' All the Law and the Prophets hang on these two commandments" (Matt. 22:37-40). Most Christians give more emphasis to the first commandment and view the Christian life primarily on the basis of their pietism, moral responsibilities, and relationship with God. Certainly a Christian's relationship with God is critical to missional disciples. However, many Christians have neglected the second commandment to love their neighbor, which includes serving their local neighborhoods, cities, and towns. Loving your neighbor is not instrumental, or a means to an end, but rather is an expression of love and worship to God. Missional disciples express love to neighbor as a witness of God's love. Building relationships with neighbors is not for the purpose of evangelism, or getting the neighbors "saved," rather it is to show their deep love for them and the community by which they live. This love is demonstrated by engaging in service to the community through community development, housing renewal, serving the elderly, working with at-risk kids, and addressing issues of hunger and homelessness. It is when community service and personal piety and action are united that persons are engaging in a holistic approach to spiritual formation.

The challenge that many Christians face is how to remain committed to their church communities while giving the time for engagement in their local communities. There is often a conflict between serving the local church and serving one's neighbor. Many Christians become insular through their participation in the local church and often do not see the value of engagement in their communities. They don't see the routine and unplanned contact with others at work, school, neighborhood gatherings, city events, and other occasions of daily life as the very places they could be working with God as ambassadors of the kingdom.[7] If Christians want to reach their neighbors, they will have to show them that they care deeply about them and the places in which they both live. It's in the particular places where Christians live that the call to mission comes.

Missional discipleship requires the practice of embodied *presence* in our community. God became flesh and dwelled among us. Jesus became one of us and lived among us. The incarnation is a reminder that Christians are to be embodied in the places in which they live and work. Christians are to enter their neighborhoods, restaurants, supermarkets, doctors' offices, and schools where broken and needy people live and where Christians can be Jesus for them. It is through this embodiment of life that Christians participate in the reign of God.

Missional communities engage their neighborhoods through a variety of practices such as raking their neighbors' leaves, providing a community garden, painting and repairing houses for the elderly, participating in local service groups, coaching soccer, providing child care, and offering food, clothing, and shelter to those in need. These activities and others are a means of grace by which the Spirit guides and leads Christians to encompass the greatest commandment to "love your neighbor as yourself."

CONCLUSION

Missional communities are led by the Holy Spirit as they discern God's working in the community and the world. It is through the community that the Spirit is active by gathering, empowering, and sending God's people to be engaged in mission. Before they can be sent into the world, God's mission begins *within* the church, the body of Christ. As Christians gather around Word and Table, God's healing mission begins. Missional communities value the church's practices as communal. Within the life of the church there are no isolated, private, and individualistic activities. Christians are formed and shaped through avenues of accountability and communal practices. Missional leaders recognize the unique gifts and abilities of all believers by encouraging them to fulfill the calling through their vocation. Also, missional communities live out their mission in local communities by loving their neighbor. They love their neighbor by serving and providing God's healing grace in the midst of pain and suffering. Living and serving in a missional community requires embodiment of *presence* as Christians go through the normal routines of life. As they are actively embodied in their communities and engaged in loving their neighbor through acts of compassion and service, they participate in the reign of God.

Discussion Questions

1. In what ways is your local congregation being a missional community?

2. How can we develop and foster missional communities? What are the benefits and challenges of missional communities?

3. In what ways is God already at work in your community? How can you find creative ways to partner with them?

4. In what ways can we apply the missional practices identified in this chapter to our local church communities?

5. How might God be calling your church community to become more missional?

6. What are the inherit challenges you face to become a missional community?

Recommended Readings

Gruder, Darrell L., ed. *Missional Church: A Vision for the Sending of the Church in North America*. Grand Rapids: Eerdmans, 1998.

McNeal, Reggie. *Missional Communities: The Rise of the Post-congregational Church*. San Francisco: Jossey-Bass, 2011.

Minatrea, Milfred. *Shaped by God's heart: The Passion and Practices of Missional Churches*. San Francisco: Jossey-Bass, 2004.

Newbigin, Lesslie. *The Open Secret: An Introduction to the Theology of Mission*, Rev. Ed. Grand Rapids: Eerdmans, 1995.

Roxburgh, Alan J., and M. Scott Boren. *Introducing the Missional Church: What It Is, Why It Matters, How to Become One*. Grand Rapids: Baker Books, 2011.

Van Gelder, Craig. *The Ministry of the Missional Church: A Community Led by the Spirit*. Grand Rapids: Baker Books, 2007.

7
THE
CODE

Teanna Sunberg
Budapest, Hungary

I AM SITTING in a sidewalk cafe on a day when the chill makes me huddle around my steaming cup of strong cappuccino. The sound of my four daughters playing with a friend's eighteen-month-old mingles with the neighboring traffic sounds, not to mention the rumble of UN peace-keeping vehicles roaring down the cobblestones. Their side-mounted machine guns should present an oddity in light of nearby children, babies, and thickly ground Turkish coffees. But long ago, we lost the ability to register any of this as ironic. These are the simple rhythms of life in this place—the spillover of cafe fellowship after believers have met in the upper room of a rented building. We will spend the afternoon here in the middle of pedestrian traffic; a community willingly visible and bound together by our mutual love for Christ.

The morning communion before our cafe fellowship was powerfully simple. I have been here when the room was cold enough to demand I keep my coat on through the entire service. One girl in our group has sacrificed simple necessities so she could pay for guitar lessons and contribute to our worship. The words projected on a nearby screen are the only evidence of a modern intrusion into this faith community. There is the Word. There is prayer. And there are kisses—left, right, left to the cheeks—both as we enter and as we depart. This is the Lord's Day: Saturday morning in one of the world's newest countries a decade after ethnic cleansing ravaged every family with the stench of death. Here in southern Europe's Balkan Peninsula, this is the Europe most people rarely envision. Yet in this place, my family and I are rediscovering the body of Christ as a profoundly transformational presence. But true transformation often exacts a high price.

As I scoot closer to catch my friend's soft-spoken words, I wonder again at what must have happened in her twelve-year-old heart when she ran for her life in the middle of the night. I adjust the position of my head so that I can scan the length of the four wobbly tables that we have pushed together to accommodate more than twenty believers. In my heart, I know that each of these young adults has his or her own story of guns and death, harrowing escapes, terror-filled border crossings, rapes, brutality, or long periods of living as refugees. How must the hardship huddling in a mountainside for survival shape how these young people think about others, about God, and about our responsibility in God's world?

Before my thoughts can take shape fully, I see our waiter in conversation with one of the new believers at our table. I quickly move to get my cash. "No," says my friend, laying her hand on mine. "He has paid the bill for all of us." I am humbled by the waiter's act of generosity and am awkward in my response. Though I do not understand the cultural nuances that have led to this moment, I recognize this new believer has acted according to an ancient moral code that remains authoritative in Balkan cultures today.

My mind flashes to a familiar story in the book of Genesis. The Lord taps his finger on the page as if to say, "This is what you have been missing." To be quite honest, I dislike the tapping finger. I hate this story. Everyone I know hates this story taken from Genesis 19 because the Sodom and Gomorrah narrative seems to make a great case for a brutal and heartless God. The story tells of how Lot offers his virgin daughters to the men of the city in order to protect his houseguests. It often becomes ammunition in anti-Christian arguments in my world. In Genesis 19:8, Lot says, "Look, I have two daughters who have never slept with a man. Let me bring them out to you, and you can do what you like with them. But don't do anything to these men, for they have come under the protection of my roof."

What kind of father is this man? Who does something like this? I can tell you: a Balkan culture does that. Balkan hospitality codes demand it. And believe it or not, this Christian lives under that roof and thanks God for this code every day.

Tragically, the deafening scream of this story and the code that surrounds me is almost inaudible to my twenty-first-century North American ears. I read this story. I watch a new believer pay our bill in the same way that I live out my Christianity; from the safety of my perspective. But in

New Testament Hospitality, John Koenig helps me begin to understand what has happened here amid the empty coffee cups on this cold Balkan day: "In the New Testament cultural tradition there was a sacred bond between host and guests, and hospitality was seen as one of the pillars of morality."[1] My new brother in Christ understands the code. Today he has put flesh on it for me. The grotesque reality of the incarnation is visibly revealed here in this story—and it takes my breath away. This is the shocking manner in which God deals with me in light of this ancient code between host and alien. I am the stranger within God's gates. I am the desperate alien—helpless, vulnerable, and unarmed against the perversions of sin that chase me through the terror-filled nights of my soul. The host has bought my rescue. God has kept the bond. God has paid the bill for all of us. From beginning to end, including this repulsive narrative in Genesis 19, this story is buried within a grander story of a tenacious God who relentlessly pursues until strangers become friends and aliens find homes.

This is the *Missio Dei*, the mission of God. Australian missiologist Michael Frost shapes this Latin phrase into a statement of God's character by stating simply: "He is the missioning God."[2] God is our host, forever on a mission. God is relentless, unstoppable, unceasingly focused on pursuit and rescue. *This* is the nature of God. *This* is God's activity: living by the very code of hospitality that runs throughout the entire story of Scripture. This promise that nothing can separate us from God's love takes on new dimensions when I read Genesis 19 over coffee with young people who have lived what it means to become refugees in the middle of too many terror-filled nights.

This is no simple story of rescue, however. It is also a story of my own responsibility because God's pursuit of me is an intentional incarnation, an intentional hospitality. The host extends himself, inconveniences himself, endangers himself, sacrifices himself to invite me in: into fellowship with him; into his kingdom; to his table; and under his roof. Then he looks at me and simply says, "Go and do likewise" (Luke 10:37). The actions of Christ speak clearly as Athanasius, one of our early church fathers, tells us: "[God] became man so that we might become godly."[3] In our world today, we are to become reflections of Christ. We become transformed into God's tangible presence and the promise of a real kingdom that acts to protect and to rescue from tragedy, addictions, genocide, human trafficking, and brokenness. The refugees among us should see a host at a table on a sidewalk with room for one more. Quite often, quite tragically, it seems that they do not.

Some would be shocked to learn that many in our world watch our neatly kept, comfortable Christianity—and label it repulsive. Repulsive? Yes, the same word I used in reference to my own view of Genesis 19. Could it be that we have cloistered ourselves so comfortably within our homes, our churches, and our neighborhoods that we are no longer available and accessible to those running through the night? Are we so keenly aware of the sinfulness of our world and so frightened by its presence that we have forgotten who has authored and continues to author our rescue? Honesty knocks. Do we have the courage to open the door and admit that we have insulated ourselves in kingdoms of our own making? Valid questions about how we live out our faith barge through the door. Do we still trust our host? Will we live by this code?

The world is waiting for us to answer. Transformation in society and within us requires sacrifice; *our* sacrifice. The only alternative is a dying Christendom. Elizabeth Newman quotes Rodney Clapp in this indictment: "Believing we have nothing distinctive to offer to 'our modern (or postmodern), democratic, capitalistic world,' the church simply 'hangs on' to Christian language but refuses to live out a genuine alternative."[4] We were born for a pivotal point in this history as voices across our planet desperately plead for rescue and redemption in the face of apocalyptic fears, colossal weather patterns, human slavery in epidemic proportions, population explosions, failing global economies, and political uncertainties. The question is whether we will submit ourselves to relearning an ancient language.

Newman offers us a beautiful invitation to live out a genuine alternative, as if we have a choice to take a risk with God. Maybe we can even push the envelope with a theologian like John Sanders, author of *The God Who Risks*, whose premise is that the Creator of the universe invites us to collaborate with God as the Father redeems all of creation. Sanders says, "The Christian faith requires a faithful God, not a risk-free God."[5] God takes a risk on us. Imagine a reality in which God's redemptive power establishes holy kingdoms of justice in war-ravaged places, and God's clarion voice pierces the dark night to lead refugees home. Dream of the God who puts on the flesh of an alien and who teaches redeemed sojourners how to guide others into safety. I am convinced that each of us longs for this dangerous journey of living out a genuine alternative. This is hospitality enfleshed.

The gift of hospitality is an intentional missioning, an intentional inclusivity, an intentional risk, an intentional choice to be the visible body of Christ in the middle of the sidewalk in a not-Christian world.

A few years ago, a young Bulgarian believer with a master's degree in chemistry felt God calling her into ministry in a Roma village where the majority of people are functionally illiterate. She left the convenience of the city and moved closer to that marginalized community. Multiple times a week, she walks almost two miles to reach villages nestled into the Balkan mountains. She eats their food served in one-room dwellings with dirt floors and no plumbing. Her people are prostitutes, pimps, kids with questionable parentages, and discarded orphans who the world will never care to know. Recently the pimp in one of her villages felt God speak to him about the sin of trafficking people for sex. In response, he dissolved his trafficking business that put food on the table for his family. He took a risk, bought some sheep, and became a shepherd overnight. Another refugee just made it home.

Quite honestly, I have lived a good portion of my life in conflict with this code. The first time I wrestled with God over my call, the biggest issue was the desire for a comfortable life in a lovely home with pleasant children and a doting husband. I wanted the American dream. My selfishness ran so deep. Yet as we moved to postcommunist Russia, God helped me face the grotesque mask of my own egocentricity in light of people who gave me everything they had, even when they had so little.

This is where I find Jesus in the repulsive beauty of a difficult Sodom and Gomorrah narrative. If we miss the essentiality of the intentional hospitality of the incarnation or if we fail to practice the gift in our context, we ourselves are lost.

The last time I traveled in the States, our family spent much time where the immigration question is a hot topic. Many of the churches we visited were somehow invested in the issue. Some congregations operated food kitchens and taught free English classes. Other churches split their Sundays to accommodate alternative ethnicities, while still others meshed into multilingual worship. Some churches got creative by sharing pastors and offering mentorships. The missiological activity was varied and congregational reaction was diverse. Some folks loved this new picture of the kingdom while others mourned the safety and homogeneity of the church that raised their kids. One sweet, retired lady who faithfully volunteered her Wednesdays to serve in the church food pantry seemed to sum up the conundrum: "We do all we can to get them into church. They come every Wednesday to the pantry and a few even stay for Wednesday night prayer, but they are not here long enough to get into a relationship with us. How do we tell them about Jesus?"

What if our pretty churches, our planned fellowship, and our compassionate outreach do not feel safe? What if programmed trendiness, upbeat music, and gourmet coffee tucked into a former strip mall or gymnasium seems more like a trap than a sanctuary? What if "Our church can be your home" friendliness seems foreign, fake, or frightening? What if our church personas, our small-group atmospheres, and our authenticated Spirit-filled vocabularies all seem incapable of fighting the real, evil-crazed mob that pounds on the door until it takes the soul? Christine Pohl most eloquently captures the nature of our current reality: "The contemporary church hungers for models of a more authentic Christian life in which glimpses of the Kingdom can be seen and the promise of the Kingdom is embodied. More than words and ideas, the world needs living pictures of what a life of hospitality could look like."[6]

What if the only way to embody the kingdom is to take a risk on God and move into Sodom and Gomorrah? Hospitality in action is a breathtaking, life-giving mixture of grace and courage. It is a reflection of the character of Christ. Now the coffee is gone. With babies sleeping and cheeks kissed, we blend one by one into the pedestrian traffic. As I walk away, a movement catches my eye and one quick glance back lets me know he is still here. Another tank thunders by and he watches it pass with squinted eyes against the setting sun. Almost absentmindedly, he fiddles with the corner of the bill. This is his way. This is his character. As the night comes, I know he will stay. He always does.

Discussion Questions

1. In what ways can we make hospitable places to connect to our neighbors and those who may be different from us?

2. What are the inherit challenges to crossing borders and being hospitable to others? Why are we reluctant to enter into these kinds of relationships?

3. In what ways are our local congregations unsafe to invite others, and how can we create a safer context that is more accepting?

4. In what ways can we incorporate intentional missional hospitality in our lives as faithful disciples of Jesus Christ? What are examples of hospitality in Scripture?

Recommended Readings

Frost, Michael. *Exiles: Living Missionally in a Post-Christian Culture.* Grand Rapids: Baker Books, 2006.

Newman, Elizabeth. *Hospitality: Welcoming God and Other Strangers.* Grand Rapids: Brazos Press, 2007.

Pohl, Christine. *Making Room: Recovering Hospitality.* Grand Rapids: Eerdmans, 1999.

Sanders, John. *The God Who Risks: A Theology of Divine Providence.* Downers Grove, IL: InterVarsity Press, 2007.

About the Author

Teanna Sunberg and her husband, Jay, serve as missionaries in the Church of the Nazarene in Budapest, Hungary. Teanna serves as the field theological education coordinator for the Central European Field. Her passion is for teaching and writing in the area of missiology. She and Jay are parents of four daughters.

8
MISSIONAL DISCIPLESHIP AND FAMILIES

Andrew Ervin
Cape May, New Jersey

WE LIVE IN A WORLD today where children and seniors are marginalized. As a society, little relative value is placed upon those on either end of the age spectrum. After all, the youngest and oldest among us are not significant producers to our economic engines, so people tend to view them differently. Why is this important to remember? Sometimes we bring this kind of thinking with us when we gather for worship, or even when we are at home interacting with our children. The church and the home are often reflections of the bigger picture in our culture. So many of our attitudes and values are shaped by what happens in our homes.

As believers, we are called to connect to the ancient way of viewing all age-groups within our family. Scripture informs us that the Law, given by God and fulfilled by Christ, was clear on the value of life. Each season and stage of life has worth. Parents were given the ultimate responsibility to be stewards of their homes and to provide spiritual leadership to everyone in their household, especially the youngest. We find this in the Shema, where among other things the Israelites were reminded, "These commandments that I give you today are to be on your hearts. Impress them on your children. Talk about them when you sit at home and when you walk along the road, when you lie down and when you get up" (Deut. 6:6-7).

In ministry today, our challenge is to enter into partnership with parents who are disconnected from older generations and often have no idea how to accomplish their responsibilities for the spiritual direction of their children. A great investment of our time and energy as church leaders requires the cultivation of an environment where families are taught. Fortunately, we can learn to ignite a movement where parents are leading the charge.

In many churches today, we do not nurture many opportunities for intergenerational conversations. This should not limit our intentional effort to still create that time. Some churches have created times they call the "family table" where faith stories are shared across age-groups. In the same way that nuclear families gather nightly at the kitchen table, church families can also gather regularly and share their intergenerational faith experiences. In this process, younger people learn their church's "family story" and older people come to appreciate the new ways that God is working among the younger generations. While this will look different from one church to another, consider looking at your weekend services and weekly offerings to see how you can create these opportunities for the family to gather and learn.

In the first chapter of 2 Timothy, Paul gives instructions to us to "fan into flame the gift of God, which is in you through the laying on of my hands. For the Spirit God gave us does not make us timid, but gives us power, love and self-discipline" (2 Tim. 1:6-7). Here he underscores that the gift of God, our salvation through Christ, our faith and life as believers, needs a "log on the fire" and some "stirring up." We call this discipleship. Here's the dilemma: many of us are not bold about accessing the power of the Holy Spirit. In fact, many of us are too timid. It's time to turn up the volume on the heat. Children's ministry leaders need to do just that, crank it up and make some noise about family discipleship.

The dictionary defines "discipleship" as "the state of being a disciple or follower in doctrines and precepts." The phrase "state of being" is usually understood as a condition or period of time, location, or place. This means that disciples need to be in learning relationships. Today this concept is often called mentoring. Mentors enter into relationships that commit to time and place. Mentors serve their protégé's best interests and care more personally about the mentored person than any content, accomplishment, or end product that might come as a result. One of my favorite quotes from my graduate work in spiritual formation was from Henri Nouwen who affirmed, "It's more about who you are becoming rather than what you are doing."

Fortunately, healthy family dynamics are prime opportunities for home mentoring relationships. Pastors are wise to encourage parents to set aside time with their entire families for talking about God. Sometimes, this can be done informally. For instance, in the car on the way to a soccer game, or at breakfast as conversations pass between the cereal boxes. These informal interactions can produce a myriad of discipleship opportunities through simple questions like, "Who can we pray for to-day?" or "Has the Holy Spirit ever put someone on your heart to invite to our church?" Practical conversation starters like these can be distributed to parents when they pick up their kids. Unfortunately, busy parents need it simple and short. Or consider placing open-ended questions on magnets for the refrigerator or create cards that can be taped to the mirror in the bathroom with a scripture and a set of questions. Key chain tags on key rings have proven effective for other family members to retain and use.

So put together a plan for how you will foster family discipleship in your home and in your congregation:

- Bible-reading tools. I heard Kurt Warner, a Christian professional athlete and philanthropist, share that he and his wife were reading the Bible together in their family room while their children were playing nearby. His son walked over to his folks and asked, "Daddy, why are you coloring your Bible?" Kurt smiled and said he was high-lighting some words that were special to him. They were teaching him something new about God. The Warner children were picking up simple, good discipleship by watching their parents read and use Bible reading tools.

- Take-home communications. Offer simple and clear scripture pas-sages, along with open-ended questions that guide and direct dis-cussion in the home. Tape them to places in the house and make them handy for use.

- Daily bread scriptures. There are a variety of Scripture devotions and cards that can be purchased, or make your own.

- Cubes and balls. Many vendors sell a variety of 3D tools for evan-gelism and discipleship. These are great for kids because they can practice communication at home with their family. Practice leading Mom to Christ again and again!

- Select a time and place. In our home we called it MAD Time or "Monday After Dinner." After dinner on Mondays, my wife, Sha-ron, and I would have our kids get their Bibles. We laid our Bibles on the kitchen table after the dishes were cleared, and then different members of our family shared a devotional each week. When our kids became functional readers and could read independently, we saw where they were at on their journeys and gave us insights as parents to how they perceived the Bible. Each week there was something new and different as our kids brought their own unique personalities to the table.

Even though there are great resources out there for connecting as a family, nothing can replace just sitting down and spending some time together. Those moments at bedtime or in the car can be valuable times for creating discipleship experiences.

One of the best things parents can do to help their children embrace the kingdom of God is to tell them their own stories of how they crossed the line of faith. This can be a powerful way for children to appreciate the importance of faith. In many significant ways, a parent's story can become a part of the child's own connection with the kingdom of God.

Discussion Questions

1. How do various age-groups tend to experience worship in your congregation?

2. How do you encourage all ages to find a place at your congregation's "family table"?

3. How do you encourage and resource your parents to have time to talk about the story of God in their homes?

Recommended Readings

Baucham, Voddie, Jr. *Family Driven Faith: Doing What It Takes to Raise Sons and Daughters Who Walk with God.* Wheaton, IL: Crossway, 2007.

Goodwin, Debbie Salter. *Raising Kids to Extraordinary Faith: Helping Parents and Teachers Disciple the Next Generation.* Kansas City: Beacon Hill Press of Kansas City, 2008.

Joiner, Reggie, and Carey Nieuwhof. *Parenting Beyond Your Capacity: Connect Your Family to a Wider Community.* Colorado Springs: David C. Cook, 2010.

Stonehouse, Catherine, and Scottie May. *Listening to Children on the Spiritual Journey.* Grand Rapids: Baker, 2010.

About the Author

Andrew Ervin is pastor to families at Seashore Community Church of the Nazarene in Cape May, New Jersey. He has served in children's ministry for over twenty years and is the author of *Best Practices of Children's Ministry: Leading from the Heart.* He has served as chairman of the Nazarene Children's Leadership Network, which holds leadership development events nationally. Andrew and his wife, Sharon, have three children.

9

HOLINESS HAS HANDS

Megan Krebs
St. Maries, Idaho

THE QUEST FOR JUSTICE as mission is a recurrent Old Testament theme, often found through the voice of prophets or Levitical laws. At times, overlooked prophets like Amos speak these truths boldly, as found in the following oracle. In Amos 5:18-27, we find a prophet of Israel with a message that is not particularly uplifting. It's actually rather tragic. In Amos 5, Israel is warned that God is sending them into exile. It's an earth-shattering revelation. Amos proclaims:

> Woe to you who long for the day of the LORD! Why do you long for the day of the LORD? That day will be darkness, not light. It will be as though a man fled from a lion only to meet a bear, as though he entered his house and rested his hand on the wall only to have a snake bite him. Will not the day of the LORD be darkness, not light—pitch-dark, without a ray of brightness? "I hate, I despise your religious festivals; your assemblies are a stench to me. Even though you bring me burnt offerings and grain offerings, I will not accept them. Though you bring choice fellowship offerings, I will have no regard for them. Away with the noise of your songs! I will not listen to the music of your harps. But let justice roll on like a river, righteousness like a never-failing stream! Did you bring me sacrifices and offerings forty years in the wilderness, people of Israel? You have lifted up the shrine of your king, the pedestal of your idols, the star of your god—which you made for yourselves. Therefore I will send you into exile beyond Damascus," says the LORD, whose name is God Almighty.

Imagine what it would be like to hear the prophet Amos speak. As a college student, I might picture it a little like this:

One day, we are all just milling about after chapel in the campus coffee shop. Summer has arrived a bit early. Outside it's blistering. So we bask in the air-conditioning, chatting. Suddenly, someone from our rival campus bursts through the door, followed by a fierce, hot blast of air. He stands in the doorway holding it open, just staring at us with eyes full of fire—they are practically glowing! His sweaty lips are pursed in disdain, bordering on contempt. Not knowing what else to do, we stare back uncomfortably—in more ways than one.

Holding the door as the furnace winds blow in, he says quietly, "God says that he hates your chapel services. They appall him. You all think you're serving God? Well, I've got news for you: this campus is about to be completely demolished!"

We would probably receive this about as well as Amos's original hearers did. After all, we're quite comfortable in our desert oasis of holiness.

It is easy for us to feel uncomfortable with this passage. First, God says to the people of Israel, "I, God, am sending you into exile." But I thought God is a God of love! Is it too late to jump ship?

Most of us are probably more than a little uncomfortable with this picture of God. We don't like the idea of a God who sends people into exile. We want to see forgiveness, not punishment. We don't like the idea of a God who gives people exactly what they deserve. We don't really want justice, at least not when it comes to us—probably because we know how badly we have messed things up.

By this point in history, the kingdom of Israel had split into two kingdoms: Israel, later called Samaria, was in the north, and Judah was in the south. And feelings of animosity and betrayal between these people rivaled the bad blood between fans of the New York Yankees and the Boston Red Sox.

The people of the northern kingdom had crafted new gods to worship and even constructed a new temple. In the eyes of Judah, their southern neighbors, they had abandoned the God who led them out of captivity in Egypt. Instead of worshiping Yahweh alone, it was as if they were collecting various action-figure gods and calling on whichever one seemed most helpful at the time. But they still considered themselves safe in the oasis of God's grace from the desert of "nonbelievers."

Now Amos enters from stage right. Amos was shepherd from a town in the south. At first, Amos declares God's judgment on neighboring countries. But this is nothing new. It's what prophets were supposed to do—point out how awful everyone else is. But God's message has an unexpected twist: now Israel is lumped together with the rest of those nations. Israel gets the same treatment as everyone else. Now the rabbit hole goes deeper, for they aren't just scolded for following other gods. This annoyingly harsh passage is where God takes off the gloves. In the verses preceding our passage, God through Amos commands the people to "seek good, not evil, that you may live. Then the LORD God Almighty will be with you, *just as you say he is*. Hate evil, love good; maintain justice in the courts" (Amos 5:14-15, emphasis added).

Up until this moment, the northern kingdom never saw them as not following God. They still burned their offerings. They were still following the laws of Moses. Israel's problem wasn't their religious observance. Today, we'd say they went to church every Sunday and chapel three times a week. Their problem was this: Israel believed their holiness only had to do with their own personal purity.

The northern kingdom had become quite wealthy and the economic gap had widened. The rich were richer and the poor were poorer. And instead of helping the needy, the religious and wealthy held them down, exploiting them in every way imaginable.

For Israel, holiness was limited to how much time they spent praying and burning sacrifices. Instead of working to right their wrongs, God's people were committing atrocities. Or they just ignored the wailings in the street. Instead of working in the world as it was, they dreamed of being spirited away on the day of the Lord. Doesn't this sound oddly familiar to our own time?[1]

Clearly, we have that same tendency. We like to define how holy we are by the things we don't do and how often we talk about God. When someone actually dares to ask us about our relationship with God, it's tempting for our responses to become a lame answer about how carefully we've attended to our daily devotions. We don't want to reach across the tracks and actually change a life—or have our own lives changed.

Not long ago, I was in San Francisco on a college field trip for a compassionate ministries course. During our time in the Bay Area, we visited several soup kitchens. We ate lunch with some of the people who passed through. To be honest, I felt pretty righteous. For a glancing moment, I thought to myself, "Aren't we great, condescending to speak with these poor people?" But then we walked outside, where I saw a woman in a faded pink sweatshirt. I don't think I will ever forget it. Her face was bloody. She pulled back from those around her as she leaned against a brick wall. The few men and women around her looked as confused and worried as I did. Then I thought frantically, "I should do something!" But in that moment I had no clue of what I should do. Instead, I stood gawking at her for a few seconds, awkwardly extending my hand out, but ultimately pulling it back again. In the same moment, others in my group were walking away. Reluctantly, I did too—looking back every few steps, fighting back tears, wishing I had done something.

What I experienced in that moment is something we all face when God asks us to put hands to our holiness. It's that feeling you get when you stare across a windy desert. Even just standing on the very edge, you can feel the sharp grains of sand hit your face as a dry, hot, unrelenting wind lashes out. It's a barren wasteland. The very ground won't hold water, and there is no escape from the unrelenting sun. It's no wonder we think that no action we take could ever make a bit of difference in the face of so many great injustices. No attitude of our hearts could ultimately matter, so why bother? "There isn't enough water in the world to quench this thirst," or so we think. No small act of kindness and no amount of money is going to amount to anything! So what's the point of pouring out a cup of water in the middle of a desert? All that does is empty my cup!

Staring into the bloody face of a homeless woman standing outside that soup kitchen, I got lost in the apparent hopelessness of the situation. So we remain silent and retreat into our little oasis of personal holiness. "I can't worry about them yet," we say. "I have to get right with God first, and then I'll go." So instead of taking our experience of God into the desert, we put our nose down and pretend there is no such thing as the desert. And we wait for Jesus to come back and get rid of all the bad people causing these problems.

We pray for forgiveness instead of justice. We pray for our oasis instead of for rain.

I suspect God was intentional in using water as the dominant image here in Amos 5. I also think it's significant that God didn't use the image of any of the large seas adjacent to Israel. While the Dead Sea and the Sea of Galilee are both fairly large—and the larger Mediterranean Sea looms to Israel's west, these bodies of water remain unmentioned in this passage. Instead God says, "Let justice roll on like a river, righteousness like a never-failing stream!"

Personally, I think a sea would have been far too overwhelming. If God had called the northern kingdom to be a sea, all they would have felt was dismay. Like us, they likely would have felt there's no way they could be that pivotal.

But here's the beauty: they didn't have to be.

Instead, God gives Amos the vision of a river. More likely, it was a picture of a stream. Deserts are vast, but people flock to the rivers and streams that flow through them. Life teems along these desert rivers; life journeys to those places where the rivers flow downstream.

A river slowly cuts away at its surroundings over time.

I also think it's significant that God confronts Israel with her sin.[2] We don't like that. I don't like that. In fact, I hate it when people point out my faults. I don't want to have them on display, and I certainly don't want to be sent into exile over them!

But God didn't just want Israel to fix their behavior. God wanted Israel to mend their hearts. God didn't ask them to save as many people as they possibly could and to overturn every unjust system. Instead, God wanted them to love their neighbors.

This isn't about behavior. It isn't about numbers or overcoming evil systems. This is about that woman in a pink sweatshirt who stands right in front of you right now. God doesn't call us to insurmountable tasks. God calls us to look at our lives and see how, with God's help, we can do small acts of wonder in our deserts. God asks us to be drops of rain.

God calls us to freedom! God wants us, and God wants us to see we aren't supposed to be so wrapped up in making sure we have our religious duties worked out that we miss out on helping our neighbors. God empowers us to be filled with love and compassion in caring for the needy around us. Not as a new religious rite but as a natural part of our life with God. Even after all these years, God still calls us to see everyone as a neighbor.

I have a friend, a fellow college student. He never has any cash because, well, because he's a college student! But it troubled him deeply that he never had any money for beggars on the street. So he prayed about it and then it hit him: now he keeps a box of granola bars in the backseat of his car. While he doesn't have much, he does have something healthy to give, and now he tries his best to have conversations with the people he meets. That's how he does justice. That's how he becomes a raindrop.

I think words like "justice" or "holiness" are lofty. Too often, they intimidate us. We instantly shirk back from these ideals. But what is holiness other than living in and through the love of God? And what is justice? It's nothing more than holiness with hands.

God has not called us to be an ocean breaking miles inland into a desert. No, God moves us to be a drop of rain in the Lord's storm.

I absolutely hate being hot. I'm one of those people who can't eat when the temperature rises. I get lethargic. Sometimes I don't even want to move.

So imagine a rainstorm with me. You can see the clouds coming from a long way off. Nothing's happened yet on the hot, dry ground. But you can see it coming. Eventually, you can feel the air pressure shift. Your arm hair starts to tingle, and your ears pop. The air has become thick with ozone; every inhaled breath feels like a fog. The rain smells earthy, moist, refreshing, like living health. Hear the rain striking the ground in sheets as it advances toward you. It hasn't hit you yet—but before a single drop arrives, you know it's coming.

Holiness with hands feels the same way. Can you sense God's love even before anything happens on the ground? We don't need to worry about watering the whole desert, that's not our job. But we can be raindrops. Christ's love is enough to saturate us with the hope given in this: God rains on us.

So with God's help, let's be rain in every dry corner of this world.

Discussion Questions

1. How does this passage from Amos shape your understanding of the *Missio Dei*? What does it say about God? About you?

2. Have you ever had a "woman in a pink sweatshirt" experience? What was it like? How did it impact you?

3. What is a practical step you could take this week in order to be a drop of rain?

4. What is a "dry place" where your group could have an impact? What is an action to which you could all commit? For example, consider shopping intentionally for a month at stores that make a positive world impact, or cut out one coffee a week and donate the saved money at the end of each month.

Recommended Readings

Brueggemann, Walter. *An Unsettling God: The Heart of the Hebrew Bible*. Minneapolis: Fortress Press, 2009.

Leclerc, Diane. *Discovering Christian Holiness*. Kansas City: Beacon Hill Press of Kansas City, 2010.

Nuffer, Bruce, Rachel McPherson, Liz Perry, and Brooklyn Lindsey. *The Kingdom Experiment*. Kansas City: House Studio, 2010.

Willard, Dallas. *The Great Omission*. New York: HarperOne, 2006.

About the Author

Megan Krebs is a Christian ministry major and pastoral ministry minor at Northwest Nazarene University. Hailing from St. Maries, Idaho, she interns at Boise, Idaho, Five Mile Church of the Nazarene.

10

GOD ON
A MISSION
A MISSIONAL THEOLOGY

Thomas Jay Oord
Northwest Nazarene University

"TODAY SALVATION has come to this house . . . For the Son of Man came to seek and to save the lost" (Luke 19:9-10).

Jesus says these words to the rich man, Zacchaeus. But we find the message repeatedly in the Bible that God seeks and saves. The missional adventure these words inspire prompts me to wonder: What would it mean to believe Jesus' loving pursuit of the lost—which seems to include you, me, everyone, and everything—tells us something essential about who God is?

This question may seem boring. But upon closer examination, I think we'll find it's revolutionary! In fact, the missional theology emerging from believing God lovingly pursues creation radically alters the status quo.[1]

The God who seeks and saves is a God on a mission!

OVERCOMING THE STATUS QUO

"Of course, God wants to save us all," someone might say. "Who would argue otherwise?"

Unfortunately, a host of theological voices in the past and present argue this way. The theology supporting these voices is sometimes hidden or unconscious. But sometimes the not-really-wanting-to-save-all God is explicitly preached.

Let's start with the easy pickings.

Those who believe God's sovereignty and election means God predestines some to hell say God doesn't want to save everyone. At least they would say God's effective will doesn't offer salvation to all. They argue for predestination, despite Peter's claim that God is "not willing that any should perish, but that all should come to repentance" (2 Pet. 3:9, KJV).

Their peculiar interpretation of this verse, in my opinion, undermines their own doctrine of divine sovereignty. I wonder, why isn't a sovereign God supposedly capable of anything also able to save all?

Those in the Wesleyan tradition walk in step with theologians who reject this view of predestination. Wesleyans, instead, affirm genuine creaturely freedom. In philosophical terms, Wesleyans affirm "libertarian" freedom.[2]

John Wesley stressed the apostle Paul's admonition to "work out your salvation with fear and trembling, for it is God who is at work in you, both to will and to work for [God's] good pleasure" (Phil. 2:12-13, NASB). Wesley passages such as this one argue that God's loving action ("prevenient grace") precedes and makes possible free creaturely responses. He advocates a theology of freedom, not predestination. This freedom has limits, of course. But it is genuine freedom nonetheless.

The God who wants to save all, however, may not actually save all out of respect for creaturely freedom. Wesleyans can affirm a missional theology that says God's intent is universal salvation. Yet they can also say universal salvation may not occur. After all, free creatures may choose to reject God's loving invitation. And God respects such decisions, despite their devastating consequences.

GOD "WANTS" TO SAVE US?

In criticizing predestination, I picked the easy fruit. I said predestinarians cannot account well for the biblical notion God wants to save us all. But let's stretch to pick some fruit less often noticed.

Many theologies—at least in their sophisticated forms—affirm an idea at odds with the missional notion God wants to seek and save. They say God lacks nothing whatsoever. God is "without passions," to use ancient theological language.

Only a needy God, say these theologians, has desires. A perfectly complete God wouldn't *want* anything. When the Bible says God *seeks* us, it isn't saying God's love desires or wants.

The Greeks called desiring love *eros*. Today, we unfortunately think of *eros* in sexual terms. But the original meaning of *eros* isn't about sex. *Eros* love might best be defined as promoting what is good when desiring what is valuable, beautiful, or worthwhile. *Eros* sees value and seeks to appreciate or enhance it.

In addition to denying divine *eros*, some theologians believe the doctrine of original sin supports their view God doesn't really have desires related to creation. Their view of original sin denies that anything good remains in creation. Sin—more particularly, the fall of Adam and Eve—left creation totally depraved, they say.

A holy God would find nothing valuable in a totally depraved world, say these theologians. In fact, God would not associate with such sinful filth. We hear this argument today, in fact, when some say a holy God cannot be in the presence of sin. A holy God, so this argument goes, cannot relate to unholy people, because sin would taint God's pure holiness.

To which I say, "Hogwash!" (or utter some other holy expletive).

Jesus Christ best expresses God's desiring love—even or especially love for filthy people. Jesus was known for hanging around unholy folk. He earned a reputation for befriending those of ill repute and ungodly character. He wanted—*desired*—those sick and broken be healed and whole.

In short, the desire for salvation we see in Jesus reflects the desire we find in God. And vice versa: the desires of God are expressed in the desires Jesus expresses in his missional life. In other words, the incarnation is our best argument that God's desires are so intense and God's love so radical "that he gave his only begotten Son" (John 3:16, KJV).

A robust missional theology, therefore, returns us to the biblical portrait of a God who desires. While God's nature is perfect and complete, God's relational experience and passionate heart include wanting something better: the restoration of God's leadership of love. God's salvation derives, at least in part, from *eros*.

JESUS WEPT

Continuing my christological focus, let's look at another important issue for missional theology: what the ancients called "divine passability."

Passability might best be described with contemporary terms like "influence," "affect," or "sway." We certainly see Jesus being influenced, affected, and swayed by others. Jesus was passable. The shortest verse in Scripture describes Jesus' passability well: "Jesus wept" (John 11:35). Matthew also reports Jesus had compassion on people, because they were "weary and worn out, like sheep without a shepherd" (9:36, HCSB). In these instances and others, we find Jesus affected by others.[3]

With skewed views of God's perfection, some theologians have said God is uninfluenced by others. God is impassable, they argue. God only influences creatures; creatures never influence God. Many classic theologies implicitly adopted Aristotle's view that God is unmoved.

This vision of an unmoved/uninfluenced/unaffected God doesn't jibe well with the Bible. The God of Scripture expresses love that both gives and receives. God loves as friend (*philia*), for instance. When believers respond well to God's love, we find God rejoicing. When they respond poorly, God is saddened, angry, and even wrathful. According to Scripture, creatures really affect God.

Today, many rightly speak of God's passability by saying our Savior is the "suffering God." This suffering was most poignant on the cross. In Christ, God suffers pain and death for the benefit of all. In fact, many theologians agree with Jürgen Moltmann and call the One who seeks and saves, "the crucified God."[4]

A suffering God—one genuinely affected by creation—is the relational God at the heart of missional theology. The influence creation has upon God does not alter God's loving nature, of course. We best interpret biblical verses saying there is "no . . . shadow of change" (James 1:17, LEB) in God as describing God's unchanging nature.

But creatures do influence the particular ways God relates to creation. Just as a perfectly loving father always loves his children, that same loving father allows his children to influence him, so he knows how best to love them in specific instances. A living God gives and receives in relationship.

To put it in missional terms, the God who seeks and saves does so to best address the specific ways we need saving! Some of us need saving from alcohol abuse; others need saving from dishonesty; others saving from unhealthy pride. God saves from all sin; but the specific ways God saves are tailor-made for creatures.

KENOSIS AND MISSION

So . . . God wants to save us all. This is God's loving desire, the divine *eros*. And the God of robust missional theology is affected by others. God is relational: both giving to and receiving from creatures. This is neither the God of predestination nor the status quo.

Now it's time to reach for perhaps the most elusive fruit of all. It's time to talk about the *power* of a missional God. We can't ignore the power issue if we want a robust missional theology. Appealing to utter mystery isn't helpful.

A number of contemporary theologians consider the Philippian love hymn especially helpful for thinking about God's sovereignty. To refresh our memory, here's the key part of that profound praise chorus:

> In your relationships with one another, have the same mindset as Christ Jesus: Who, being in very nature God, did not consider equality with God something to be used to his own advantage; rather, he made himself nothing by taking the very nature of a servant, being made in human likeness. (2:5-7)

Theologians often focus on the Greek word *kenosis*, which is translated here "made himself nothing." Other translators render *kenosis* "emptied himself" or "gave of himself." These translations suggest that Jesus does not overpower or totally control others. Instead, Jesus reveals God's servant-style power.

Kenosis suggests divine self-limitation. The Bible says Jesus reveals God's very nature in this *kenosis*, because Jesus expresses limited power, like a servant.

Perhaps it's best to say God empowers rather than overpowers. After all, empowering describes servant-style influence better than overpowering or total control. And empowering fits the notion that creatures possess some measure of freedom to respond well or poorly to God. Presumably, God grants power/agency to creatures to make freedom and agency possible. God is our provider.

There are two main ways to talk about God's self-limitation revealed in Jesus. The first and more common is to say self-limitation is voluntary on God's part. This view says God *could* totally control and overpower others. But God voluntarily chooses not to be all-determining—at least most of the time. The voluntary self-limitation model says God *could* totally control others, however, should God so decide.

The main problem with the voluntary divine self-limitation model is the problem of evil. The God who *could* overpower those who inflict genuine evil *should* in the name of love. To put it another way, the God who voluntarily self-limits should become un-self-limited to rescue those who suffer needlessly. At least in some cases, God should become un-self-limited to seek and save the lost. Voluntary divine self-limitation cannot provide a satisfactory answer to why God doesn't prevent unnecessary pain, suffering, and death.

The other way to talk about God's limited power Jesus reveals says God's self-limitation is involuntary. It is self-limitation, in the sense that no outside force or factor imposes constraints on God. But it is involuntary, in the sense that God's power of love derives from God's own nature.

Because God is love, God never overpowers others. In love, God necessarily provides freedom/agency to others and never completely controls them. God's loving nature compels God to empower and never overpower others. We might call this "essential kenosis."

John Wesley endorses involuntarily self-limitation in one of his sermons: "Were human liberty taken away, men would be as incapable of virtue as stones," Wesley argues. "Therefore (with reverence be it spoken) the Almighty himself *cannot* do this thing. He *cannot* thus contradict himself or undo what he has done" (emphases added).[5] God must be God, says Wesley, and God's nature of love involves giving freedom/agency to others.

Although often unnoticed, the Bible offers examples of things God cannot do (e.g., God cannot lie; God cannot tempt). In my view, however, these examples fall under the general category expressed in Paul's words: "[God] cannot deny himself" (2 Tim. 2:13, KJV). God's power as involuntary self-limitation says God controlling others entirely—coercion—would require God to deny God's loving nature. And that's impossible . . . even for God.

Of course, affirming involuntary divine self-limitation requires new thinking about doctrines of creation, miracles, and eschatology. But these doctrines can still be affirmed: God is still Creator, miracle-worker, and hope for final redemption. They may need recasting, however, in light of God's persistently persuasive love. Such recasting is not new to Wesleyans, because they typically try to propose Christian doctrines in light of divine love.[6]

The main point of this section, then, is that the power God exercises in the missional adventure to seek and to save the lost is persuasive power. Missional theologians may prefer one form of divine self-limitation over another. But they together affirm that God's power operates through love. God's kenotic love, revealed in Jesus, is primarily if not exclusively the power of persuasion. God calls instead of controls.

Those called to missions—which includes us all—ought to follow the kenotic example of Jesus: we should express empowering, relational love.

FREE, FREE, SET THEM FREE

"The Spirit of the Lord is on me," said Jesus. Standing in his hometown temple, he continues reading a passage from Isaiah: "he has anointed me to proclaim good news to the poor. He has sent me to proclaim freedom for the prisoners and recovery of sight for the blind, to set the oppressed free, to proclaim the year of the Lord's favor" (Luke 4:18-19).

Among the many ways biblical authors talk about God seeking and saving, the themes of healing and freedom from oppression appear often. Healing and deliverance are part of the well-being/abundant life/favor the Lord generously offers. And we desperately need the well-being—*shalom*—of God's salvation.

In a world of brokenness, wholeness breaks in. This wholeness is evident in the local church I attend, in which a robust Celebrate Recovery ministry has emerged. Those in this group believe God empowers them to overcome hurts, habits, and hang-ups. God is their deliverer. Through this and other avenues in the church, many find God's healing and deliverance.

The apostle Paul says liberation comes from the Spirit and becomes effective through Jesus. "The law of the Spirit of life in Christ Jesus has set you free from the law of sin and death," he says (Rom. 8:2, LEB). In this liberation, we see God again empowering us in ways that provide salvation from destruction.

A look at the overall scope of Scripture leads one to believe humans are the focus of God's seeking and saving. But the Bible also says God cares about nonhumans.[7] In fact, Scripture says God intends to redeem *all* things. The whole creation hopes to be "set free from its bondage to decay and will obtain the freedom of the glory of the children of God" (Rom. 8:21-22, NRSV).

We play a vital role in this mission. We can be co-laborers with God's work for the redemption of all things. God acts first to call, empower, and guide us in love—prevenient grace. But God seeks our cooperation. This becomes clear in the *Revised Standard Version*'s translation of Romans 8:28: "We know that *in everything* God works for good *with* those who love him" (emphases added).

We can work for good *with* God. The healing and deliverance God has in mind involves our participation.

LOVE IS ON THE MOVE

A God on a mission is a God on the move. And love is the primary and persistent intent of our God-on-the-move. A robust missional theology is a theology of love.

To love is to act intentionally, in response to God and others, to promote overall well-being.[8] God's initial and empowering action makes response possible. We live in community with others to whom we also respond. We are not isolated individuals, and God desires the common good.

God's love establishes God's kingdom—or what I call God's loving leadership. Here again, it is through Jesus we believe such things. Jesus preached God's loving leadership as both possible and actual here in this life. And he proclaimed its fulfillment in the life to come.

As a young child, I learned a chorus I now sing to my kids. It derives from 1 John 4:7-8: "Beloved, let us love one another, for love is from God; and everyone who loves is born of God and knows God. The one who does not love does not know God, for God is love" (NASB). John says our best clue about what love entails is this: God sent Jesus.

The God who seeks and saves is revealed best in Jesus Christ. This God of love desires that all creation live shalom. God works powerfully through love to fulfill this desire, and we are invited to join in this love project. The result is the healing, restoration, and liberation of all held captive to sin and death. This holy God—revealed best in Jesus' life, death, and resurrection—is on a mission of love.

John takes these truths about God, love, and Jesus a bit further and concludes with this logic: "Since God loved us so much, we also ought to love one another" (4:11, NRSV). Thankfully God makes love possible, says John: "We love because he first loved us" (4:19). The empowering God enables us to love.

A missional theology supporting the endeavor to seek and save the lost is not based primarily on an evangelistic canvassing strategy. Nor is it based primarily upon duty and obedience to God. It's not even based primarily upon worship. Strategies, obedience, and worship are all important. But missional theology is based primarily on love.

We ought to "follow God's example, . . . as dearly loved children and walk in the way of love, just as Christ loved us" (Eph. 5:1-2a). This missional ethic emphasizes generosity, listening and speaking, both influencing and being influenced by, enabling, mutuality, and community. It's a strategy that cares for the least of these and all creation.

In short: God loves us, and we ought to love one another. We ought to imitate God's full-orbed love—*agape, eros,* and *philia*—as we cooperate with God's mission to seek and save the lost.

The God on a mission invites us on an adventure of love.

Discussion Questions

1. In your opinion, what in the theological status quo needs to be changed?

2. How important is it that creatures are genuinely free and the Creator is not in complete control?

3. What does it mean for discipleship to believe God empowers rather than overpowers?

4. What does it mean to say we can and should imitate God by living lives of love?

Recommended Readings

Boyd, Gregory. *God of the Possible.* Grand Rapids: Baker Books, 2000.

Clayton, Philip. *Transforming Christian Theology: For Church and Society.* Philadelphia: Fortress, 2009.

Montgomery, Brint, Thomas Jay Oord, Karen Winslow. *Relational Theology: A Contemporary Introduction.* San Diego: Point Loma Press, 2012.

Oord, Thomas Jay. *The Nature of Love: A Theology.* St. Louis: Chalice, 2010.

_____, and Michael Lodahl. *Relational Holiness: Responding to the Call of Love.* Kansas City: Beacon Hill Press of Kansas City, 2005.

_____, and Robert Luhn. *The Best News You Will Ever Hear.* Boise, ID: Russell Media, 2011.

About the Author

Thomas Jay Oord is professor of theology and philosophy at Northwest Nazarene University. He is the author or editor of over a dozen books, including *Relational Theology*; *The Nature of Love: A Theology*; and *Defining Love: A Philosophical, Scientific, and Theological Engagement*. He is known for his contributions to research on love, relational theology, science and religion, and Wesleyan theology. He and his wife, Cheryl, have three daughters.

11

LIVING
WORDS
READING THE BIBLE AS SCRIPTURE

Richard P. Thompson
Northwest Nazarene University

WYSIWYG. No, you have not suddenly slipped into a different language or encountered the exclamation of a terror-stricken child after seeing an ugly-looking bug in the bathroom! In the early days of personal computing prior to Apple/Mac and Windows platforms, the text that was typed on a computer screen often looked very different from what ended up on the printed page. So the acrostic WYSIWYG, which stood for "What You See Is What You Get," helped computer users determine whether or not a particular program allowed them to preview a page prior to printing it. Today we do not give such matters a second thought, as most programs convert whatever appears on the computer screen to match what we print.

Although the dynamics change a bit when we move from word processing or textual composition on a computer to reading words on a page, the principle "What You See Is What You Get" still applies. And this is especially true when it comes to reading the Bible! For as both our observation of others' practice and our own experience attest, we all seem to read the Bible with some sort of purpose in mind. That is, we all have particular hopes and expectations that we bring with us when we open the Bible and read the words on the page. If we would admit it (at least to ourselves), those purposes and expectations—even the theology and Christian experiences that shape us as believers—all contribute to the unique lenses through which we read and interpret these biblical texts. And such things direct our attention as we read the Bible to such an extent that "what we see is what we get." So if we read the Bible to confirm ideas we already hold, then we should not be too surprised when we come away with precisely that. Or if we approach the Bible as a database of theological information and instruction, then the end results will be measured by what information and principles have been gleaned and learned from the respective biblical text.

Of course, there are many other ways of reading the Bible that have their rightful place among the optional approaches to biblical interpretation. However, the concern here is not merely for reading the *Bible*, because doing so is not necessarily the same thing as reading *Scripture*.

Christians from various walks of life and with vastly different abilities in biblical interpretation have all experienced the difference between the two, when they have read a passage from the Bible and hoped to hear a message from God through those written words, only to close the cover after a while to perceived divine silence. Yet often our approach to reading the biblical texts has more than a little to do with whether these written words also become *living words* in our contemporary contexts, which would indicate that indeed we are reading and listening to sacred Scripture. So that is our focus here: to think about how we may go about reading and interpreting the Bible faithfully as *Scripture*, which (among other things) listens and seeks for divine purpose and guidance (transformation and call to action) *through* the biblical texts.[1] Such an approach may also be called "missional biblical hermeneutics" because it focuses on what the true essence of Bible reading should be: "the missional path of God"[2] that those who are theological heirs of John Wesley would understand in terms of God's purposes of salvation (not only conversion but also including the Christian life). In particular, three aspects to reading the Bible as Scripture need to be considered more closely.

First, the church is the privileged context for the interpretation of the Bible as Scripture. Although biblical materials (such as the Ten Commandments) are often suggested to be authoritative for all people or are read more individualistically, a quick scan of the biblical texts themselves may lead to a different conclusion: the original, primary addressees of the biblical texts are those who may be designated as "the people of God" (Israel in the Old Testament; the church in the New Testament). These materials address their readers in various ways to help form and shape them as God's people, to instruct them how to treat one another as God's people, and to guide them in their dealings with other peoples. They told different stories driven by their theological purposes for the community of faith rather than by interests in preserving historical details per se (see, e.g., Deut. 6:20-25; Luke 1:1-4; John 20:30-31). We find that even the nature of the Christian canon itself has the implicit understanding of the church as the location both for the reading and interpretation of the biblical texts. By the end of the second century AD and long before official ecclesiastical decisions about the canon (Council of Carthage; AD 397), most of what now makes up the New Testament, along with the Old Testament, had already been functioning authoritatively as sacred Scripture in the life of the early church by speaking into and about her worship, faith, practice, and being. So these texts remain on the table to the present day with a standing invitation for the church to read them, listen to them, and reflect upon them again, not simply as static historical documents for a different time but as sacred texts to which the Christian tradition has consistently revisited.[3]

While today's readers may not fully recognize or appreciate all the specific historical concerns of a given passage, the hope is that a fresh reading will shape the church's faith and practice.[4] If the church is to be faithful to her identity and to avoid mirror reading (i.e., reading their own agendas and needs into the biblical text), substantive critical work is needed to engage the biblical texts in contemporary settings due to the "otherness" of these texts in terms of time, place, and the like.[5] At the same time, the church must listen in ways that imaginatively consider how these texts may continue to speak. After all, it is inevitable that the text will speak differently to a contemporary context much different from its original one.[6] Still, the church is the interpretive context assumed by the notion of Christian canon where an "integrative act of the imagination" occurs, in which the church places her faith and practices imaginatively within the world presented by those texts.[7] Such creative readings mirror the ways that texts often functioned in the ancient world and that the canonical texts functioned within the church through her history. Thus, in order for us to read the Bible as Scripture, the privileged context for such reading and interpretation must be the church.

Second, the essential component for the interpretation of the Bible as Scripture is the inspiration of the prayerful church by the Spirit of God. The church is not left to her own creativity or devices when it comes to interpreting the Bible. At the same time, one should not assume that the Bible has inherent qualities that make it authoritative or enable it to function automatically as Scripture.[8] While the Christian church affirms divine inspiration of the biblical texts in terms of authorship, such affirmations do not guarantee the Bible that contemporary readers hold in their hands will speak directly and clearly about their particular life situations, or to them. Nor do such beliefs in a divine inspiration from the past ensure that we might hear biblical challenges that might actually speak against ourselves today. However, although 2 Timothy 3:16-17 is often cited to affirm the inspiration of the biblical authors, we should note that this passage's description of Scripture (in this instance, a reference to the Old Testament) as "God-breathed" or "inspired" (NRSV, CEB; *theopneustos*) actually does not point to the past (i.e., to a moment of writing) at all. Rather, the description of divine inspiration in this important biblical text is parallel to Scripture's *present* function as being "useful" for several of the church's formative tasks ("teaching, rebuking, correcting and training in righteousness"). Therefore, as John Wesley insightfully comments on this verse, "The Spirit of God not only once inspired those who write it, but continually inspires, supernaturally assists, those that read it with earnest prayer."[9] That is, it takes the ongoing activity of God's Spirit, within the context of the church that is prayerfully dependent upon God, to breathe new life into the words of the biblical text and to make them a fresh message from God for a new day. Otherwise, these words from an ancient era will remain lifeless and insignificant for the contemporary church. None of our well-meaning declarations about the Bible in our hands as "the inspired word of God" will make them speak as God's word to us. Only the Spirit of God, working actively and *presently*, can speak through ancient texts so they become *living words* that overcome the barriers of time and culture to address those whom God has called to be the church (note: *ekklēsia*, "the called ones").

Such a dual understanding of inspiration enables contemporary readers to engage the biblical texts in ways that are both historically responsible and spiritually sensitive so as to listen to them as sacred Scripture. On the one hand, readings of the Bible that emphasize only the inspiration of the biblical authors often tend to minimize the historicity of the biblical texts. For instance, claims that "God had us in mind when God inspired the biblical authors" ignore major language and cultural considerations that are part of the biblical texts and must be taken seriously as part of the interpretive task. On the other hand, readings of the Bible that assume divine inspiration to be a "one and done" event ensuring the given biblical text with inherent divine qualities do not account for the applicability of that same text in contemporary contexts shaped by very different assumptions about the universe, the social order, and human nature. However, an understanding of inspiration by God's Spirit within the context of the church enables the biblical text to function as Scripture so that God may address and shape the contemporary church as the people of God *through* it.

Third, the expected confirmation of the interpretation of the Bible as Scripture is the outcome of faithful response or the performance by faithful interpreters of Scripture. A significant indication that the church is interpreting the Bible as Scripture may be seen in her reception of and response to these texts in various aspects of her ongoing life as the church. When Jesus followed up an aspect of his teaching by stating, "Anyone who has ears to hear should listen!" (Mark 4:9, 23; Luke 8:8; 14:35, HCSB; cf. Matt. 11:15; 13:9, 15, 43), the command "listen" stressed the need not only to pay attention but also to *obey* them (as the verb *akouō* often connotes). When the apostle Paul wrote a letter to a church, the expectation was that the letter would initiate responses of faithfulness on the part of those Christians who read and engaged his articulation of the gospel that addressed their situation. Even biblical narratives, whether they are of God's deliverance of Israel or the Gospels, tell these stories to shape the people of God in distinct ways and to evoke faithful response in times very different from those narrated events. One could say that these examples all have a common assumption: that these biblical materials are somehow "incomplete" in themselves, apart from the outcome of faithful response. That is, the general expectation behind biblical materials, certainly if we are to read them as Scripture, is that there is more to the interpretive task than merely the *rearticulation* of a possible meaning of a given passage: a new set of words that explains what the old set of words (i.e., the biblical text) meant. Rather, when the church engages the biblical texts as sacred Scripture, she does not simply talk about what these texts may say but instead actively responds in faithful ways to the God about whom these texts speak and who speaks to her through them. Such response, inspired by the Spirit's activity within the church, makes these texts *living words* as the church embodies them in her ongoing life.

A helpful way of thinking about this approach to interpreting Scripture is what may be called "performance interpretation."[10] Like a script of a play or a musical score that is expected not merely to be studied but to be performed, so too does Scripture have similar expectations. All three assume that there will be some degree of faithfulness to what has been provided as a guide for the accompanying performance, but that some element of improvisation will also contribute an interpretive aspect to each performance, with the result that no two performances will be the same. And even these events and activities of performance are not mere results of interpretation but vital to the interpretive process, as we learn something in the very act of performance. Thus, we perform Scripture and thereby embody it and interpret it afresh in the rituals of the church, in her ministries, and in her creative, missional embodiment of the love of God within the world.[11] In so doing, we actually come to know God more fully. As one old saying goes, "We may be the only Bible that some people will ever read." And so it is, when we truly embody Scripture as *living words* that have been given life by God's Spirit, we live as the missional people of God and take on the very character of God.

Both in the pew and behind the pulpit, people often cite (either directly or indirectly) the descriptions found in Hebrews 4:12 when thinking about the Bible: "For the word of God is alive and active." Although this passage actually does not refer to the Bible per se but more generally to *whatever* way God chooses to speak, we can affirm that something happens when the Bible becomes sacred Scripture. That is, something happens when the words on the pages of our Bibles take on new life among and through those identified as the church because the Spirit of God inspires them to embody and perform what they engage in these texts.[12] But for many of us, this requires a change in how we approach our reading and interpretation of the Bible. One cannot begin with the assumption that the words on the page will automatically speak today. Sermons will need to give more attention to calls of corporate action. And Bible studies cannot be content with gaining a "better understanding" of a given passage but will need to intersect with the mission of the church. However, by reading so that the Bible might become Scripture, we open ourselves so that these words become *living words*, both in our prayerful reading and in our faithful performance. May it be so!

Discussion Questions

1. What are some different ways that we read the Bible? Or some different reasons for reading the Bible? To what extent do you agree with the author's assessment that "What you see is what you get" when it comes to reading the Bible? Explain.

2. Do you agree or disagree with the view that the interpretation of the Bible as *Scripture* belongs to the church? What about the use of selected passages of Scripture like the Ten Commandments in settings outside the church (e.g., in a courtroom setting)? How does one account for the individual Christian who reads Scripture privately for devotions? Why is the faith community *still* the privileged context for interpreting the Bible as Scripture?

3. When most of us speak of the Bible and inspiration, to what do we refer? How does that understanding compare with and/or differ from the view of inspiration that John Wesley affirmed? And how might this Wesleyan understanding of inspiration help us view and read the Bible differently today?

4. What comes to your mind when you consider the idea that the nature of the biblical materials themselves may make these texts "incomplete"? How does this relate to the concepts of inspiration that this essay proposes? And in what ways do such understandings of response and performance depend on related views of God, God's grace, and the transformation that comes through God's grace?

5. How does the metaphor of performance help in thinking about the interpretation of the Bible as Scripture? How would you compare the interpretation of the Bible to the performance of a play or musical score? In what ways might the concept of improvisation in such contexts provide insight metaphorically into what happens when the Bible becomes Scripture?

Recommended Readings

Callen, Barry L., and Richard P. Thompson, eds. *Reading the Bible in Wesleyan Ways: Some Constructive Proposals.* Kansas City: Beacon Hill Press of Kansas City, 2004.

Fowl, Stephen E. *Engaging Scripture: A Model for Theological Interpretation*, Challenges in Contemporary Theology. Malden, MA: Blackwell, 1998. Reprint, Eugene, OR: Wipf and Stock, 2008.

Green, Joel B. *Seized by Truth: Reading the Bible as Scripture.* Nashville: Abingdon, 2007.

McKnight, Scot. *The Blue Parakeet: Rethinking How You Read the Bible.* Grand Rapids: Zondervan, 2008.

Wright, N. T. *Scripture and the Authority of God: How to Read the Bible Today.* New York: HarperOne, 2011.

About the Author

Dr. Richard P. Thompson is professor of New Testament and chair of the Department of Religion in the School of Theology and Christian Ministries at Northwest Nazarene University in Nampa, Idaho. He is a graduate of Olivet Nazarene University and Nazarene Theological Seminary and earned his Ph.D. in Religious Studies from Southern Methodist University.

He has pastoral experience in three different churches and has written or edited six books in addition to numerous journal articles and book essays.

12

THE RIPPLE EFFECT

HOW THE LOCAL CHURCH CAN CHANGE THE WORLD THROUGH MISSIONAL PARTNERSHIPS

Joe Gorman
Northwest Nazarene University

"If anyone has material possessions and sees a brother or sister in need but has no pity on them, how can the love of God be in that person? Dear children, let us not love with words or speech but with actions and in truth. . . . Whoever claims to live in [God] must live as Jesus did."
—1 John 3:17-18; 2:6

"Christ has no body now on earth but yours, no hands but yours, no feet but yours, yours are the eyes through which he looks with compassion on this world, yours are the feet by which He is to go about doing good, yours are the hands by which He is to bless us now."
—St. Teresa of Avila

AS CHRIST'S DISCIPLES we are called to embody the love of God not only "with words or speech but with actions and in truth" (1 John 3:18). When we act with Christlike compassion by feeding the hungry, giving a cup of clean water to the thirsty, loving the stranger, clothing the naked, and visiting those who are sick or in prison (Matt. 25:31-46), we make visible the love of God in the world. Living out the Christian life in missional ways has been a vital part of our Wesleyan tradition since its earliest days. John Wesley was insistent upon this when he invited early Methodists to "join hands with God to make a poor man live."[1] As Phineas Bresee, one of the founders of the Church of the Nazarene, exhorted, "We are indebted to give the gospel to every [person] in the same measure in which we have received it."[2] Following in the wake of such a compelling biblical and theological heritage, missional discipleship in the twenty-first century will lead us to take up our crosses and follow Jesus into the forgotten corners of the world, living compassionately and offering resurrection hope among the wounded, vulnerable, and underserved.

In June 2001, when I was the pastor of Golden Church of the Nazarene in Golden, Colorado, I started traveling to Nairobi, Kenya, each summer to teach a few courses in the religion department at Africa Nazarene University. While at ANU I met students from several African countries with whom I became fast friends. As these students graduated with their degrees and returned to their home countries as pastors and later district superintendents, they asked me to visit their families and local churches. During my visits I preached and taught, but mostly listened and observed as I followed my friends around while they engaged in various ministries. Wanting to encourage them and their projects, I asked how my church could partner with them. They told me the biggest need of their local churches was to start animal rearing projects. If my church in Golden could help them purchase a few goats, ducks, and chickens, it would help them feed the handful of children they were ministering to in Sunday school and a small school during the week. While this wasn't the kind of ministry I was used to, my small church gladly raised a couple hundred dollars to get these projects off the ground.

What my church and I didn't know at the time was that we were developing what those in the community development field call global partnerships or, what we are calling in this chapter, missional partnerships. At the time we weren't worried about naming what we were doing. We were simply trying to be good friends, to treat these global neighbors of ours as we would want to be treated if we were in their place. The few goats, ducks, and chickens provided by one local church to another have now expanded to include other holistic ministry projects, such as building schools and toilets, digging wells, providing sewing machines for widows with HIV/AIDS, starting pig-raising businesses to educate at-risk girls, creating literacy programs, providing housing for widows and orphans, and developing sustainable businesses and agricultural projects for handicapped men and women. In all these projects we come alongside local pastoral leadership to help others help themselves, to give opportunities that their context simply does not allow. By giving a hand up rather than a hand out, we seek never to do what others can do for themselves, thus promoting self-sufficiency and long-term sustainability.

HOLISTIC LOVE OF NEIGHBOR

Ministry in Africa and my Wesleyan theological tradition have confirmed for me that the good news of Jesus is holistic. As we participate in God's mission in the world, we seek the renewal of all things in Christ by working for mental, social, material, and spiritual flourishing. This is nothing less than the biblical notion of shalom: peace with God, our neighbors, and the environment. The kingdom of God thus embraces both the saving of souls and the unleashing of the saving health of God in Christ for the whole person.

John Wesley understood Christ's ministry to the physical needs of people not merely as a potential vehicle leading to salvation, but as integral to Christ's saving work. Ministry to the physical and spiritual needs of people was inseparable for him. Wesley, for example, collected food for the hungry, visited prisoners, helped the poor help themselves, established schools for children, provided clean water, clothes for cold bodies, medicine for the sick, hospitality to the imprisoned, assisted the weak and sick by building medical clinics, and gave microloans to start small businesses.[3]

As I join hands with my African friends in compassionate ministry, they challenge me to be thoroughly incarnational. When they talk about evangelism, for example, they never mention conversion to Christ apart from talking about education, health, clean water, or an ongoing source of income that meets basic human needs and provides meaning for life. Loving our neighbor in a Wesleyan spirit certainly includes evangelism, as we typically think of evangelism, but it is not limited to it. Caring compassionately for our neighbor also involves tending to spiritual, physical, emotional, relational, and economic needs.

Evangelism in a Wesleyan spirit demonstrates compassion for the entire person; for, if only the spiritual matters, then food, water, shelter, health, jobs, and education are incidental to the gospel. Separating life into spiritual and unspiritual compartments could not be further from the gospel Jesus embodied or Wesley preached, however. Compassion is thus not something we do in addition to or instead of evangelism, but is itself fundamental to the good news Jesus preached and lived.[4] Since prevenient grace permeates all of human life, breaking down the walls between secular and sacred distinctions, missional discipleship recognizes and seeks to make Christ known in every aspect of human life.

WALKING AS JESUS WALKED

The basis of missional partnerships is the imitation of Christ. Following Christ's example was the driving force of John Wesley's ministry in eighteenth-century England. Christ was not only Wesley's model for ministry to the most vulnerable but also the source of its empowerment. The motivation for Wesley's ministry was to walk as Jesus walked (1 John 2:6).[5] "Why did Wesley work with the poor?" Richard Heitzenrater asks, "because Jesus did so, but also because Jesus told him to do so and would help him to do so."[6] Wesley's passion for the poor, in following the pattern of Jesus' life, lasted throughout his long lifetime. When Wesley was eighty-two years old, for example, he spent a week slogging through the melting snow and muddy streets of London "begging" for the poor. As a result of about thirty hours spent soliciting funds that week, he raised two hundred pounds, or the equivalent of around $30,000 in today's currency.[7]

Unlike for Wesley, the poor for us are not only the poor who live next door or in big cities in North America, Europe, or the United Kingdom. They are also the global poor. These poor are the 3.5 billion (half the world's population) in developing countries who live on less than $2.00 per day.[8] The average household income in America is about $135 per day, however.[9] Most of the people I've worked with in Rwanda, Democratic Republic of Congo, and Ghana live on less than $1.00 per day. It's nearly impossible to support oneself and family on $2.00 per day, let alone $1.00 per day, even in a developing world context. In the developing world, families must pay for the costs of their children's education, including school fees, school supplies, school uniforms, exams, and so forth. Yes, things tend to cost much less in such countries than in our own Western context, but it's simply impossible to feed, shelter, clothe, and educate adequately a family anywhere on $1.00 per day. In war-torn eastern Democratic Republic of Congo, for example, a chicken can cost $10.00 and a single papaya $1.00. As a result of struggling to provide their families even the basic necessities of life, far too many children, and especially girls, never have the opportunity to attend school. A heartbreaking number of children don't even receive basic caloric requirements, often leading to stunted brain development, a compromised immune system, and even death. Following Christ into missional discipleship will lead us to do the same things Jesus did: living compassionately, loving children, and sharing our resources with others.

WHO IS MY NEIGHBOR?

In his book *The World Is Flat*, Thomas Friedman describes how developments in technology, the Internet, and worldwide interconnectivity have "flattened" the world in the last twenty years.[10] These developments, along with the increasing ease and affordability of worldwide travel, make communication possible with global neighbors almost as if they live next door to us. In previous years our response to the question the expert in the Law posed to Jesus in Luke 10:29, "And who my neighbor?" would be those who live closest to us and are most like us culturally, socially, economically, and religiously. Today, however, our neighbor may live next door or in a mud, grass-thatched hut in Ghana. In light of our access to instant communication and awareness of the plight of our global neighbors, we can no more turn our backs on them than John Wesley could ignore the poor, hungry, sick, and uneducated children on the streets of eighteenth-century London.

The flattening of the world makes it possible and necessary for the body of Christ to be Christ's hands reaching across the globe to the most vulnerable. When we develop missional partnerships that connect the resources of the developed world with the needs of the majority world, we partner with our global brothers and sisters as if they live across the street from us. In our globally interconnected world, the practice of the early church in

Acts 2 where "all the believers . . . sold property and possessions to give to anyone who had need" (vv. 44-45), takes on new meaning for us. In a world where we often spend money on things we don't need, it makes sense that we consider part of our calling as missional disciples to steward our money intentionally in order to make a significant and enduring global impact that builds for the kingdom of God and saves lives.

JESUS, LIVING WATER, AND WELLS

What do missional global partnerships look like in practice? One example of the holistic ministry we've been talking about comes from the life of my friend, Rev. Frank Mills, who is a pastor and district superintendent in the Church of the Nazarene in Ghana. Frank, a Ghanaian national, preaches about Jesus as living water in conjunction with a well dug by local labor in partnership with a church in the United States. The well's water is free to all in the community: Christians, Muslims, and animists. As Pastor Frank says, "As God's grace in Christ is free to all, so is access to clean water. We have found that clean water often leads people to the living water of Christ."

While clean water is a global health problem, it's also a spiritual issue. Access to clean water fosters health and saves lives. Wells give children time to attend school. Wells provide women more time to earn an income and be with their children. Wells deliver clean water that enables children, men, and women to live fuller, more productive lives. One of the best ways to share the reality of the living water of Christ is through clean, accessible water. The shalom (wholeness, wellness, holistic peace) that Christ brings is for the healing of every facet of our lives: spirit, mind, body, emotions, and relationships. As Christians we believe that clean water promotes health and saves lives that God created in love. Jesus said, "Whatever you did for one of the least of these [such as giving the thirsty a drink of clean water], you did for me" (Matt. 25:40).

A single well in a rural area services around a thousand people a day. The statistics regarding the need for clean water in the majority world are mindboggling to those of us who simply turn a faucet on and expect clean, hot and cold water to flow instantly:

- One in seven people in the world (one billion people) do not have access to clean water.
- Unsafe water and a lack of basic sanitation cause 80 percent of all disease.
- More people die from water-related diseases than from all forms of violence, including war.
- Every fifteen seconds a child dies somewhere of a water-related illness. This amounts to the deaths of six thousand children every day, or the equivalent of twenty jumbo jets crashing daily. If twenty commercial airliners crashed every day, we'd all be outraged and demand that something be done immediately to correct the situation.[11]

In developing countries, women and girls often spend four or more hours every day carrying water in bright yellow jerricans because they don't have local access to water. Long hours spent carrying water prevents many girls in such countries from attending school and prevents their mothers from earning an income. Imagine what your life would be like if you had to spend half your workday carrying water or if your daughter could not attend school because she needed to fetch water for your family.

As important as statistics are in conveying metrics for measuring the gravity of particular problems, there is nothing like a story to put faces on potentially mind-numbing numbers. When I was in Ghana this last summer, I asked some of the people in Galenzewu, a rural, arid village in north central Ghana, how the well Compassion for Africa sponsored in their community has helped their lives. A woman with a baby on her back told me before the well was dug she walked three to four hours a day to fetch water. She expressed heartfelt thanks that God has used the Church of the Nazarene to bring clean water to her village. She said not only has she received spiritual help from Christ as her "living water," but the water from the well has cut down problems of cooking, bathing, and washing clothes. Life is much better for her now, she says, because her children are healthier and experience diarrhea much less frequently. Galenzewu's village chief told me, "Water is everything. When a guest visits my compound, I offer water even before food. What does your visitor think if you offer him dirty water? Now I am proud to have guests and offer them clean water." Another man pointed out, "In Christ there are many blessings. Water was a very big problem for us before the Church of the Nazarene came to our village. We had to travel very far for water and the people near the water made us pay for it even though cattle drank from it and defecated in it. As a result, many of our children got diarrhea, ringworm, and died." Since the digging of the well, however, the people in Galenzewu are healthier and fewer children are dying.

One cup of clean water will not change the entire world, but it can change the world for the one on the receiving end. Missional discipleship starts by asking God how we can live out the compassion of Christ in the world and then by taking even one faltering step to do something rather than nothing.

EDUCATE A GIRL, CHANGE THE WORLD

Another concrete example of how we can partner with global communities in holistic compassion is to help educate at-risk girls. The logic here is very simple: educate a girl, change the world. Nicholas Kristof and Sheryl WuDunn's wonderful book and now PBS documentary, *Half the Sky: Turning Oppression into Opportunity for Women Worldwide*, explores the role of women in changing the world as well as the conditions restricting the development of women. The phrase "half the sky" comes from a Chinese proverb that says women hold up "half the sky." Advocating for girls' education grows out of the theological affirmation that God created us in his image, male and female. God clearly intends that both women and men fulfill the purpose for which God has created us in Christ.

One very concrete way for individuals and churches to participate in God's mission in the world is to provide educational opportunities for girls in developing countries where one out of three girls is not educated past fourth grade. Imagine that you have three girls of your own and must choose which one of them will not attend school past the fourth grade. Or, imagine that you have nine girls in your Sunday school class or youth group, but only three out of the nine can go to school past fourth grade. Even though such choices for us in the developed world are nearly impossible to comprehend, they are an everyday reality for many in the developing world.

A little education goes a long way in helping girls help themselves. When a girl in the majority world receives seven or more years of education, she marries four years later, has 2.2 fewer children, less health complications, and is less likely to contract HIV/AIDS. An extra year of primary school boosts girls' eventual wages by 10 to 20 percent. Every year of secondary school lifts girls' earning capacity 15 to 25 percent. Research in developing countries has also shown a consistent relationship between better infant and child health and higher levels of schooling among mothers. Further, when women and girls earn income, they reinvest 90 percent of it into their families while only 30 to 40 percent of men do the same.[12]

The compassionate ministry of district superintendent Frank Mills in northeastern Ghana, near the border of Burkina Faso and Togo, provides another outstanding example of missional discipleship in action. The accounts of his ministry often read as if they were coming from the pages of the New Testament or the journals of John Wesley. Three years ago Frank and his wife, Hanna, started a pigs for young girls project that gives adolescent girls in northeastern Ghana a pair of pigs as a living savings account. As the pigs multiply and are sold, they provide income for the girls' school fees, uniforms, and supplies. Girls in northeastern Ghana who don't have such income-generating projects are often "sold" into polygamous marriages to men who are twice or even five times a young girl's age.

Most fathers in rural northeastern Ghana view their daughters as property to be sold rather than as a precious life to be loved and nurtured. They do not see the point of educating a daughter they will eventually "sell off" to the highest bidder in an arranged marriage (marriages in this

140

context are based upon economic arrangement rather than a relationship of love). Fathers reason something like, "I'll get two cows for my daughter when I give her to be married. She'll only get pregnant and work in the field the rest of her life, so why should I spend *my* money for her to go to school when the man who becomes her husband doesn't want an educated wife anyway?" Most men in northern Ghana don't want educated wives, as they believe educated wives give them too much trouble. Such are the "poor, nasty, brutish, and short" lives of too many girls and women in rural northern Ghana.

When I was in northeastern Ghana this past summer, I asked several of the young teenage girls involved in the Wilbur Project, "What would life be like for you now if you had not received a pair of pigs?" Their responses were virtually identical: "By now I would have been given to an old man in marriage and given birth to at least one baby with another one on the way. My life would be miserable. I would have no choices for my future and very little hope." Because of Frank Mills' heart of compassion, over two hundred girls—who would have otherwise become teenage mothers (some as young as fourteen years old) and ended up working a harsh and unforgiving life as the third or fourth wife on their husband's cocoa or maize farm—are still in school. Two hundred may not sound like a lot in the total scheme of things, but if we imagine: "Any of these girls could be my daughter, granddaughter, or sister," it puts their well-being in a completely different light.

Together as the body of Christ, each of us doing what we can, locally and globally, with what we have, where we are, partnering with God for the renewal of the world in Christ, truly can unleash a ripple effect of change one girl, one boy, one family, one village at a time.

WHAT YOU CAN DO

Here are some ideas to get you and your church started in developing compassionate missional partnerships:

1. Give what you can. By slowly cutting back on unnecessary purchases in your life, you can change the world for a boy or a girl or even save his or her life.

   "Once the commitment is clear, you do what you can, not what you can't. The heart regulates the hands" (2 Cor. 8:12, TM).

2. Raise funds for the causes about which you are passionate. It may be that your resources or those of your church are limited (none of us are Bill and Melinda Gates), but you may know others who have significant resources. We often underestimate the reach of our compassion because we think only in terms of our own bank account. Even if you yourself don't have a lot of money to give, you can hold a fund-raiser and tell others about the projects for which God has placed a burden on your heart.

   "Give a loaf of bread yourself; someone else can give a cup of wine, and another clothes. In this way, you can relieve one man's poverty by your joint effort" (Gregory of Nyssa, fourth century).

3. Sponsor a child. You can do this individually, as a Sunday school class, children's ministry, youth group, or church. No matter what the size of our bank account, every person and church can do something. As Wangari Maathai, the late Nobel Peace Prize laureate from Kenya, was fond of saying about seemingly small efforts, "Remember the story of a hummingbird that tries to put out a forest fire. When mocked by other animals, the hummingbird replies, 'I'm doing what I can.'"

4. Become a student of the causes you care about and then share what you learn with others. Read the books and visit the websites listed at the end of this chapter and give to the charities they represent. You can be a direct link between your church, family, friends, and the needs of the global community.

5. Use Facebook, Twitter, and other social media to share stories and pictures about those who are engaging in Christlike compassion in the world.

6. Serve on a short-term mission trip. When short-term mission trips are done well, they mutually enrich those served and those who serve. They also change us and our perspective regarding the needs of those in the majority world.

7. Form missional partnerships in your community with the most vulnerable. While the needs of those in developing countries are often desperate, there are refugees, the unemployed, the underemployed, and the underserved right outside our doors. When discerning a call to serve the needy, it's most often not an either/or, but a both/and call to serve, locally and globally.

8. Do not make the mistake of thinking, "Since I can't do everything I won't do anything." This is a huge mistake, because the truth is: by the grace of God you and I can do something, however small or insignificant it may seem. We may not be able to do everything, but each of us can do something. None of us can change the world by ourselves, but together with God we can change the world one girl, one boy, one family, one village at a time.

    "If you think you are too small to make a difference, try spending the night in a closed room with a mosquito" (African proverb).

9. Pray. As an African proverb says about the relationship between prayer and practice: "When you pray, move your feet."

Discussion Questions

1. What concrete steps can you, your church, Sunday school class, small group, children's ministry, or youth group take to form a missional partnership with another church somewhere in the developing world?

2. How can you and your family make your financial gifts to God's mission in the world more personal? Brainstorm with your family

small but meaningful steps for making a personal connection with an at-risk child somewhere in the world.

3. What obstacles (theological, financial, personal, etc.) are preventing you from serving your neighbors near and far with Christlike compassion?

4. As a missional disciple, where and how is God calling you to "join hands with God" in serving those who are most vulnerable?

5. Where can you cut back on unnecessary expenses so you can give more generously to Christian organizations engaged in holistic ministry?

Recommended Readings

Kristof, Nicholas D., and Sheryl WuDunn. *Half the Sky: Turning Oppression into Opportunity for Women Worldwide*. New York: Alfred A. Knopf, 2009.

Myers, Bryan L. *Walking with the Poor: Principles and Practices of Transformational Development*. Revised and Expanded Edition. Maryknoll, NY: Orbis Books, 2011.

Singer, Peter. *The Life You Can Save: How to Do Your Part to End World Poverty*. New York: Random House, 2009.

Stearns, Richard. *The Hole in Our Gospel: The Answer that Changed My Life and Might Just Change the World*. Nashville: Thomas Nelson, 2009.

Stone, Bryan P. *Compassionate Ministry: Theological Foundations*. Maryknoll, NY: Orbis Books, 1996.

Internet Resources

"Compassion for Africa." www.compassionforafrica.org.

"The Girl Effect." www.girleffect.org.

"Half the Sky Movement." www.halftheskymovement.org.

"Nazarene Compassionate Ministries." www.ncm.org.

"World Vision." www.worldvision.org.

About the Author

Dr. Joe Gorman is associate professor of pastoral theology and director of the undergraduate Online Christian Ministry program at Northwest Nazarene University. He is also the executive director of Compassion for Africa, a 501(c)(3) organization that engages in sustainable compassionate ministry projects in Africa. He was the senior pastor of Golden Church of the Nazarene in Golden, Colorado, for almost twenty-one years.

EPILOGUE
IN SEARCH OF A
BETTER FLASH MOB

Jay Richard Akkerman
Northwest Nazarene University

THIS PAST DECEMBER, my wife was talking with a fellow teacher at her high school. It was the last day of the semester. Both students and teachers were eager for their long-expected Christmas break. As they talked about their respective holiday plans, Kim's colleague offered some "insider information" regarding a flash mob that was being organized the next afternoon at the large regional mall in our community.

If you're not familiar with flash mobs, they are a relatively recent phenomenon. On the surface, these groups of people seem to gather for a spontaneous public performance and disperse after a few brief minutes. *Chambers Dictionary* defines a flash mob as "a group of people who arrange to assemble briefly in a public place to perform some activity, often of a humorous or surreal nature."[1] They seem to have found their place in popular postmodern history, thanks in part to the flexibility of cellular communications. As Ian Urbina notes in a 2010 article in the *New York Times*:

> It started innocently enough seven years ago as an act of performance art where people linked through social-networking Web sites and text messaging suddenly gathered on the streets for impromptu pillow fights in New York, group disco routines in London, and even a huge snowball fight in Washington.[2]

According to the classified information Kim received that Friday December afternoon, her colleague had schemed to join other musicians from her church at noon the next day. They planned to surprise Boise's busy holiday shoppers by assembling as a flash mob at the base of the food court escalators where they were going to sing "The Hallelujah Chorus" from Handel's *Messiah*.

Along with our three teenaged daughters, we were eager to take in Saturday's surprise spectacle. After all, Kim and I had sung "The Hallelujah Chorus" many times before, during, and after college. We've also seen other flash mobs perform Handel's Christmas classic online. Some are spectacular. Secretly, we hoped this might be a story we'd be weaving into our family's holiday lore well into the future.

I underestimated the vehicular congestion we encountered in the mall parking lot that Saturday, so Kim, the girls, and I arrived at the top of the food court escalators a couple of minutes past noon. Lots and lots of people were milling around. But no one was singing.

When I looked down on the escalator's center court, I saw the problem: four uniformed security guards, complete with flat-brimmed Smokey the Bear hats[3] perched on their heads, had discovered the flash mob's plot before it was fully hatched. Everything was now at a standstill as the head security guard questioned the conductor and awaited permission from mall management about whether the orchestra and choir members would be permitted to perform. More and more holiday shoppers gathered with us on the rail of the upper deck to witness the stalled performance below.

Apparently Kim's friend and her church group tipped their hand prematurely, which took some of the "flash" out of their mob. Rather than having one clandestine, unaccompanied soloist burst seemingly into spontaneous song with Handel's bold hallelujahs, then growing voice by voice, this church group assembled on the floor as a horde. They dragged in metal folding chairs, an electric keyboard on a long umbilical, and about a dozen rickety music stands. Choir members each carried a full fan of sheet music in their hands. Even the drowsiest mall cop could have seen this group assembling from a mile away. What should have been a four-minute performance, followed by an immediate dispersion of the musicians back into the crowd, dragged into a forty-minute waiting game with dismayed shoppers ultimately chanting, "Let them sing! Let them sing!" in exasperated unison.

When it appeared the growing crescendo of customers might soon get out of hand, the beleaguered security head took matters into her own hands and waved for the group's conductor to get on with it. Many in the crowd cheered, while still others groaned over the long, drawn-out process. After a few more awkward moments, the musicians then proceeded to tune up their instruments. Finally the singers commenced, while some shoppers on the rail—Kim and me included—even sang out our parts of the chorus from memory. In a few minutes, we belted out Handel's final "Hallelujah!" together in fairly triumphant harmony.

As the flashless mob began folding up their tottering music stands and packing away their instruments, Kim and I ambled down the mall concourse with our kids. Just then, I heard one disillusioned passerby comment, "That seemed more like a flush mob than a flash mob!"

Our misadventure reminded me how those of us in the Christian mob can turn flashes into flushes. Most of the time, we really have the best intentions. But if we're not careful we can do the right thing for the wrong reason. Or we do it the wrong way and communicate a very different message to those who gather in our midst.

Compare my family's Christmas mall experience with that of some Catalonians sauntering about on a Saturday evening roughly seven months earlier:

> On May 19th at six in the evening, what appeared to be a single, tuxedoed street performer playing a bass for people strolling around Plaça de Sant Roc in Sabadell, Spain (just north of Barcelona) turned into a mass ensemble performing a movement of Beethoven's Ninth Symphony—including more than 100 musicians and singers from the Orchestra Simfònica del Vallès, Amics de l'Òpera de Sabadell, Coral Belles Arts, and Cor Lieder Camera.[4]

Trust me: before reading another word on this page, you really need to go online and see this four-minute YouTube clip for yourself.[5] Classical music fans know this piece as Beethoven's final symphony,[6] those in the European Union sing it as their national anthem, but most churchgoers recognize it as the tune accompanying Henry van Dyke's enduring hymn "Joyful, Joyful, We Adore Thee."[7]

As seen in the video, a solitary street musician emerges initially out of a frozen pose after a young Spanish girl drops a coin into his top hat. The soloist's performance soon becomes a duet, grows into a quartet, then an ensemble, and ultimately swells into a choral symphony. Cellos, violins, and bassoons quickly meet with horns, clarinets, timpani, and what appears to be a rousing, randomly amassed choir.

Trent Gillis correctly reminds his readers, "Let's make no mistake here; this is a commercial for Banco Sabadell. And, yes, it's a majestic, highly orchestrated flashmob organized by one of Spain's largest banking groups."[8] But the piece's musical and video production quality pales in comparison to the wondrous expressions seen on the faces of those passing by. From a father with his son hoisted on his shoulders, to an elderly woman heading home from the market, to small Spanish children straining to see over the crowd or whirling feverishly to the strains of the orchestra, to a young strolling mother entranced by the music with her infant in tow, this ad hoc musical experience leaves Catalonians both young and old beaming and breathless.

It's not merely the difference in musical quality that differentiates the summer flash mob at Plaça de Sant Roc from the Christmas flush mob at Boise Towne Square. It's also about the degrees to which the musicians succeeded in engaging their audiences with intentionality and ultimately invited them to participate fully in the performance with them. It's also about how one group of performers emerged seamlessly out of the population's ranks and then melded back into the crowd. One experience transformed an audience full of passersby into inspired participants. The other experience left too many on the perimeter simply feeling flushed.

All I know is that the little girl outside the Banco Sabadell sure got her money's worth.

As missional disciples, I hope we'll offer the same value to our world.

NOTES

Prologue

1. "Pedestrian Counts," Times Square. http://www.timessquarenyc.org/do-business -here/market-facts/pedestrian-counts/index.aspx. Website.

2. Charles V. Bagli, "Audit Criticizes 1998 Deal by City for Times Sq. Hotel," *New York Times*, February 12, 2013, http://www.nytimes.com/2013/02/13/nyregion/marriott -marquis-deal-could-cost-taxpayers-344-9-million-audit-says.html (accessed March 29, 2013).

3. John Portman & Associates, Project Description, http://www.portmanusa.com/proj ectdescription.php?name=New%20York%20Marriott%20Marquis&projectid=5626 &sector=&csector= (accessed June 17, 2012).

4. James Traub, *The Devil's Playground: A Century of Pleasure and Profit in Times Square* (New York: Random House, 2004), 153.

5. Steven Kurutz, "John Portman, Symphonic Architect," *New York Times,* October 19, 2011, http://www.nytimes.com/2011/10/20/garden/john-portman-symphonic-architect-qa .html (accessed June 17, 2012).

6. Traub, *Devil's Playground*, 153.

Chapter 1

1. Dean G. Blevins and Mark A. Maddix, *Discovering Discipleship: Dynamics of Christian Education* (Kansas City: Beacon Hill Press of Kansas City, 2010), 17.

2. See Milfred Minatrea, *Shaped by God's Heart: The Passion and Practices of Missional Churches* (San Francisco: Jossey-Bass, 2004).

3. Benjamin T. Conner, *Practicing Witness: A Missional Vision of Christian Practices* (Grand Rapids: Eerdmans, 2011), 22.

4. Alan Hirsch and Debra Hirsch, *Untamed: Reactivating a Missional Form of Discipleship* (Grand Rapids: Baker Books, 2010), 29.

5. Kenda Creasy Dean, *Almost Christian: What the Faith of Our Teenagers Is Telling the American Church* (New York: Oxford Press, 2010), 93.

6. Blevins and Maddix, *Discovering Discipleship*, 211-12.

7. David and Gabe Lyon Kinnaman, *Unchristian: What a New Generation Really Thinks about Christianity, and Why It Matters* (Grand Rapids: Baker Books, 2012), 26.

Chapter 2

1. Anthony B. Robinson, *Called to Be Church: The Book of Acts for a New Day* (Grand Rapids: Eerdmans, 2006), 43. "All churches that dedicate themselves to Christian formation and to growing people of faith must find ways for students to become teachers, for disciples to move on and become apostles sent into the world to minister in Christ's name."

2. "Mission Possible," http://www.mission-possible.ca/.

3. "Heal the Kids Project," http://healthekidsproject.wordpress.com/.

4. "The Parent Support Group for Families of Mentally Handicapped Adults Society," http://www.members.shaw.ca/parentsupport/.

5. "SA Foundation," https://safoundation.com/sa_foundation.

6. The phrase "for the life of the world" is inspired by Alexander Schmemann, *For the Life of the World: Sacraments and Orthodoxy*, 2nd rev. and expanded ed. (Crestwood, NY: St. Vladimir's Seminary Press, 1982).

7. Richard P. Heitzenrater, *Wesley and the People Called Methodists* (Nashville: Abingdon Press, 1995), 299. "The Methodists did not have to look for strangers to find the poor."

8. Theodore Jennings Jr., *Good News to the Poor: John Wesley's Evangelical Economics* (Nashville: Abingdon Press, 1990), 57.

9. http://nazarene.org/files/docs/LeadersResponses03.pdf.

Chapter 3

1. Walter Rauschenbusch, *A Theology for the Social Gospel* (Guernsey, GY, United Kingdom: HardPress Publishing, 2012).

2. Lesslie Newbigin, *The Open Secret: An Introduction to the Theology of Mission* (Grand Rapids: Eerdmans, 1995).

3. Brian McLaren, *A Generous Orthodoxy* (Grand Rapids: Zondervan, 2006), 107.

4. N. T. Wright, *How God Became King* (San Francisco: HarperOne, 2012).

5. Greg L. Hawkins and Cally Parkinson, *Reveal: Where Are You?* (Chicago: Willow Creek Association, 2007).

6. Frank's website can be found at: http://www.klpx.com/page.php?page_id=17.

7. Bill Hybels and Lynn Hybels, *Re-Discovering Church* (Grand Rapids: Zondervan, 1997).

8. Lewis Rambo, *Understanding Religious Conversation* (New Haven, CT: Yale University Press, 1993).

Chapter 4

1. Ed Stetzer and Thom S. Rainer, *Transformational Church: Creating a New Scorecard for Congregations* (Nashville: Broadman and Holman, 2010), 1.

2. Marva Dawn, *The Sense of the Call: A Sabbath Way of Life for Those Who Serve God, the Church, and the World* (Grand Rapids: Eerdmans, 2006), 13.

3. Eugene Peterson, *Christ Plays in Ten Thousand Places: A Conversation in Spiritual Theology* (Grand Rapids: Eerdmans, 2005).

4. D. Michael Henderson, *Making Disciples: One Conversation at a Time* (Kansas City: Beacon Hill Press of Kansas City, 2007).

5. James W. Fowler, *Stages of Faith: The Psychology of Human Development and the Quest for Meaning* (San Francisco: HarperCollins, 1976).

6. Reggie McNeal, *The Present Future: Six Tough Questions for the Church* (San Francisco: Jossey-Bass, 2003), 73.

7. Mark A. Maddix and Richard P. Thompson, "The Role of Scripture in Christian Formation," in *The Bible Tells Me So: Reading the Bible as Scripture*, ed. Thomas Jay Oord and Richard P. Thompson (Outskirts Press, 2011), Kindle Locations 3148-3149.

8. Paul Sheneman, *Illuminate: An Advent Experience* (Kansas City: Beacon Hill Press of Kansas City, 2011).

9. Kerry and Chris Shook, *One Month to Live: Thirty Days to a No-Regrets Life* (Colorado Springs: WaterBrook Press, 2008).

10. Fowler, *Stages of Faith*, xiv.

11. Mark A. Maddix, "The Life of Spiritual Formation Defined," in *Spiritual Formation: A Wesleyan Paradigm*, ed. Diane Leclerc (Kansas City: Beacon Hill Press of Kansas City, 2011), Kindle Locations 95-96.

12. Richard Rohr, *Falling Upward: A Spirituality for the Two Halves of Life* (San Francisco: John Wiley and Sons, 2011), Kindle Locations 688-690.

13. Fowler, *Stages of Faith*, 210.

Chapter 5

1. Chris Folmsbee, *A World Unbroken: Hope and Healing for a Shattered World* (Kansas City: Barefoot Ministries, 2011), 9.

2. Brad Brisco, *God's Mission Is Ours* (Kansas City: House Studio Blog, 2012).

3. John R. W. Stott, *Christian Mission in the Modern World* (Downers Grove, IL: InterVarsity, 1975), 23.

4. Jürgen Moltmann, *The Church in the Power of the Spirit: A Contribution to Messianic Ecclesiology* (London: SCM Press, 1977), 64.

5. Jon Huckins and Rob Yackley, *Thin Places: 6 Postures for Creating and Practicing Missional Community* (Kansas City: House Studio, 2012), 32.

6. Tim Milburn, *Equip* (Kansas City: Barefoot Ministries, 2012), 82.

7. Ibid.

8. Andrew Root, *Revisiting Relational Youth Ministry: From a Strategy of Influence to a Theology of Incarnation* (Downers Grove, IL: InterVarsity Press, 2007), 15.

9. Alan Hirsch and Lance Ford, *Right Here, Right Now: Everyday Mission for Everyday People* (Ada, MI: Baker Books, 2011), 68-69.

10. Ibid.

Chapter 6

1. Darrell Gruder, ed., *Missional Church: A Vision for the Sending of the Church in North America* (Grand Rapids: Eerdmans, 1998), 144-45.

2. Lesslie Newbigin, *The Gospel in a Pluralistic Society* (Grand Rapids: Eerdmans, 1989), 223.

3. Blevins and Maddix, *Discovering Discipleship*, 22-23.

4. Darrell Gruder, ed., *Missional Church: A Vision for the Sending of the Church in North America* (Grand Rapids: Wm. B. Eerdmans, 1998), 155-56.

5. Mark A. Maddix, "The Biblical Model of the People of God: Overcoming the Clergy/Laity Dichotomy" in *Christian Education Journal* 6(2), 2009, 218.

6. Lesslie Newbigin, *The Gospel in a Pluristic Society* (Grand Rapids: Wm. Eerdmans, 1989), 234.

7. Roger Helland and Leonard Hjalmarson, *Missional Spirituality: Embodying God's Love from the Inside Out* (Downers Grove, IL: InterVarsity Press, 2011), 176-77.

Chapter 7

1. John Koenig, *New Testament Hospitality: Partnership with Strangers as Promise and Mission* (Philadelphia: Fortress Press, 1985), 16.

2. Michael Frost and Alan Hirsch, *The Shape of Things to Come: Innovation and Mission for the 21st Century Church* (Peabody, MA: Hendrickson Publishing, 2003), 43.

3. Brian M. Lipfin, *Getting to Know the Church Fathers: An Evangelical Introduction* (Grand Rapids: Brazos Press, 2007), 290.

4. Elizabeth Newman, *Untamed Hospitality: Welcoming God and Other Strangers* (Grand Rapids: Brazos Press, 2007), 23.

5. John Sanders, *The God Who Risks: A Theology of Divine Providence* (Downers Grove, IL: InterVarsity Press, 2007), 196.

6. Christine Pohl, *Making Room: Recovering Hospitality* (Grand Rapids: Eerdmans, 1999), 10.

Chapter 9

1. Douglas Stuart, "Amos," in Word Biblical Commentary: *Hosea-Jonah*, Vol. 31, ed. David A. Hubbard, Glenn W. Barker, and John D. W. Watts (Waco, TX: Word Books, 1987), 274-400.

2. This concept of confrontation as blessing stemmed from a conversation with NNU's Old Testament professor, Professor Stephen Riley (Ph.D. candidate). A great many thanks go to him for this conversation and many others.

Chapter 10

1. For a short and accessible introduction to the gospel of love, see the evangelistic book I cowrote with Robert Luhn, *The Best News You Will Ever Hear* (Boise, ID: Russell Media, 2011).

2. The distinction about forms of freedom is necessary, because some predestinarians say they affirm creaturely freedom but also the idea God alone decides the chosen few who will be saved. They are, to use the philosophical language, "compatiblists," at least when it comes to issues of salvation.

3. For an accessible theology of holiness from a relational perspective, see the book I wrote with Michael Lodahl, *Relational Holiness: Responding to the Call of Love* (Kansas City: Beacon Hill Press of Kansas City, 2005).

4. Jürgen Moltmann, *The Crucified God: The Cross of Christ as the Foundation and Criticism of Christian Theology* (Philadelphia: Fortress, 1993; New York: HarperCollins, 1991; London: SCM, 1974).

5. John Wesley, "On Divine Providence," Sermon 67, *The Works of John Wesley*, vol. 2 (Nashville: Abingdon, 1985), paragraph 15.

6. See Thomas Jay Oord, *The Nature of Love: A Theology* (St. Louis: Chalice, 2010).

7. For an exploration of a Wesleyan doctrine of creation, see Michael Lodahl, *God of Nature and of Grace: Reading the World in a Wesleyan Way* (Nashville: Kingswood, 2003).

8. I explain the details of this definition from philosophical, scientific, and theological perspectives in my book, *Defining Love: A Philosophical, Scientific, and Theological Engagement* (Grand Rapids: Brazos, 2010).

Chapter 11

1. Joel B. Green, *Seized by Truth: Reading the Bible as Wesleyans* (Nashville: Abingdon, 2007), 3-6.

2. Scot McKnight, *The Blue Parakeet: Rethinking How You Read the Bible* (Grand Rapids: Zondervan, 2008), 105.

3. Max Turner, "Historical Criticism and Theological Hermeneutics of the New Testament," in *Between Two Horizons: Spanning New Testament Studies and Systematic Theology*, ed. Joel B. Green and Max Turner (Grand Rapids: Eerdmans, 2000), 57 ff.

4. Cf. Robert W. Wall, "The Significance of a Canonical Perspective of the Church's Scripture," in *The Canon Debate*, ed. Lee Martin McDonald and James A. Sanders (Peabody, MA: Hendrickson, 2002), 529-31.

5. Stephen E. Fowl, *Engaging Scripture: A Model for Theological Interpretation*, Challenges in Contemporary Theology (Malden, MA: Blackwell, 1998; reprint, Eugene, OR: Wipf and Stock, 2008), 75-83.

6. Cf. Trevor Hart, "Tradition, Authority, and a Christian Approach to the Bible as Scripture," in Green and Turner, *Between Two Horizons*, 196; Stephen B. Chapman, "Reclaiming Inspiration for the Bible," in *Canon and Biblical Interpretation*, ed. Craig G. Bartholomew et al. (Grand Rapids: Zondervan, 2006), 183.

7. Richard B. Hays, *The Moral Vision of the New Testament: A Contemporary Introduction to New Testament Ethics* (San Francisco: HarperSanFrancisco, 1996), 6. Cf. Green, *Seized by Truth*, 72-79.

8. See Richard P. Thompson, "Authority Is What Authority Does: Rethinking the Role of the Bible as Scripture," in *The Bible Tells Me So: Reading the Bible as Scripture*, ed. Richard P. Thompson and Thomas Jay Oord (Nampa, ID: SacraSage, 2011), 43-56.

9. John Wesley, *Explanatory Notes upon the New Testament* (London: Epworth, 1958), 794.

10. See, e.g., Shannon Craigo-Snell, "Command Performance: Rethinking Performance Interpretation in the Context of Divine Discourse," *Modern Theology* 16.4 (October 2000): 475-94; and Michael G. Cartwright, "The Practice and Performance of Scripture: Grounding Christian Ethics in a Communal Hermeneutic," *Annual of the Society of Christian Ethics* (1988): 31-53.

11. Cf. Richard B. Hays, *Echoes of Scripture in the Letters of Paul* (New Haven, CT: Yale University Press, 1989), 191: "No reading of Scripture can be legitimate, then, if it fails to shape the readers into a community that embodies the love of God as shown forth in Christ."

12. Cf. Stephen E. Fowl and L. Gregory Jones, *Reading in Communion: Scripture and Ethics in Christian Life* (Grand Rapids: Eerdmans, 1991; reprint, Wipf and Stock, 1998), 20, who insist an indispensable standard for evaluating biblical interpretation is faithful living before God: "One cannot begin to judge whether this standard is being achieved unless and until the interpretation of Scripture becomes socially embodied in communities of people committed to ordering their worship, their doctrines, and their lives in a manner consistent with faithful interpretation."

Chapter 12

1. John Wesley, "A Plain Account of the People Called Methodists" (1749), in *The Bicentennial Edition of the Works of John Wesley*, ed. Albert C. Outler (Nashville: Abingdon Press, 1987), 9:280. Hereafter abbreviated as BCE.

2. Cited by H. Orton Wiley in the Introduction to Donald Brinkley, *Man of the Morning* (Kansas City: Nazarene Publishing House, 1960), http://wesley.nnu.edu/fileadmin/imported_site/wesleyctr/books/Other/Bresee%20Package/HDM3385.pdf (accessed March 1, 2013).

3. Wesley, "Plain Account of the People Called Methodists," in *BCE*, 9:272-80. See especially p. 279, footnote e: loans for microenterprises were not to exceed five pounds, or about $750 in today's currency.

4. See Tom Nees, *Compassion Evangelism: Meeting Human Needs* (Kansas City: Beacon Hill Press of Kansas City, 1996).

5. As Richard Heitzenrater points out, this was "the most repeated biblical phrase (over fifty references) in his published sermons." See Richard Heitzenrater, "The Imitatio Christi and the Great Commandment: Virtue and Obligation in Wesley's Ministry with the Poor," Chapter 3, in *The Portion of the Poor*, ed. M. Douglas Meeks (Nashville: Kingswood Books, 1995), 58.

6. Ibid., 63.

7. Richard Heitzenrater, "The Poor and the People Called Methodists," in Chapter 1, *The Poor and the People Called Methodists*, ed. Richard Heitzenrater (Nashville: Kingswood Books, 2002), 31, 223.

8. According to 2008 figures from the World Food Bank, 70.9 percent of the population in Southeast Asia lives on $2.00 a day or less; 69.2 percent of the population of Sub-Saharan Africa lives on $2.00 a day or less. See http://data.worldbank.org/topic/poverty (accessed February 16, 2013).

9. *The Economist*, "Cutting the cake: The real incomes of America's richest and poorest households," September 14, 2011. See http://www.economist.com/blogs/dailychart/2011/09/us-household-income (accessed February 16, 2013).

10. Thomas L. Friedman, *The World Is Flat: A Brief History of the Twenty-First Century* (New York: Picador/Farrar, Straus and Giroux, 2007).

11. For more information regarding the need for clean water, see http://www.unicef.org/media/media_45481.html, http://www.who.int/water_sanitation_health/wsh0404summary/en/, http://hdr.undp.org/en/reports/global/hdr2006/, http://www.unicef.org/health/index_51412.html (accessed February 19, 2013).

12. The above statistics come from a compilation of research by the World Health Organization, UNICEF, and other organizations and can be found at www.girleffect.org. Kristof and WuDunn give numerous examples of how education is changing the lives of girls and communities in the majority world in *Half the Sky*. See especially Chapter 10, "Investing in Education," 167-78. More information can be found at the *Half the Sky* website: www.halftheskymovement.org.

Epilogue

1. *Chambers Dictionary*, 11th ed., s.v. "Flash Mob."

2. Ian Urbina, "Mobs Are Born as Word Grows by Text Message," *New York Times*, March 24, 2010, http://www.nytimes.com/2010/03/25/us/25mobs.html?_r=0 (accessed March 25, 2013).

3. U.S. Department of Agriculture, "The True Story of Smokey Bear" (Western Publishing Co., 1960), http://files.dnr.state.mn.us/forestry/wildfire/prevention/smokey/comic book.pdf (accessed March 26, 2013). Cover.

4. Trent Gilliss, "Flashmob or Polished Ad on a Spanish Plaza, This Video Is a Feast," On Being with Krista Tippett, July 2, 2012, http://www.onbeing.org/blog/flashmob-or-polished-ad-spanish-plaza-video-feast/4740 (accessed September 7, 2012).

5. View the clip in high definition at http://youtu.be/GBaHPND2QJg.

6. Maev Kennedy, "Beethoven's Ninth Manuscript Could Fetch £3m," *The Guardian*, April 8, 2003, http://static.guim.co.uk/sys-images/Guardian/Pix/arts/2003/04/08/9th.jpg (accessed March 27, 2013).

7. Henry Van Dyke, "Joyful, Joyful, We Adore Thee," http://www.docstoc.com/docs/418516/joyful-joyful-we-adore-thee (accessed March 26, 2013).

8. Gilliss, "Flashmob or Polished Ad on a Spanish Plaza."

More books by
MARK A. MADDIX

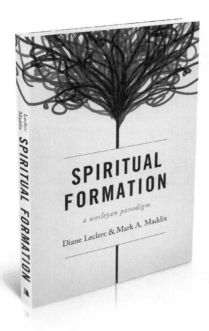

People have a deep hunger and thirst for something that transcends them. This book focuses on how people can grow in Christlikeness while also providing guidance on self-care, spiritual direction, and mentoring.

Spiritual Formation
by Mark A. Maddix, Diane Leclerc
ISBN: 978-0-8341-2613-8

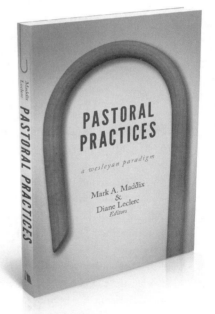

Whatever the task may be—preaching, discipling, evangelizing, or administrating—this book sheds light on the way Wesleyan theology refines, informs, and enhances the theories and methods of each pastoral practice.

Pastoral Practices
Mark A. Maddix, Diane Leclerc (Editors)
ISBN: 978-0-8341-3009-8

BEACON HILL PRESS
OF KANSAS CITY

Available online at BeaconHillBooks.com